CHICAGO COOKS

Enjoy this small
Taste of history!

Carl M. Haffer

CHICAGO COOKS

25 Years of Food History with Menus, Recipes, and Tips from Les Dames d'Escoffier Chicago

Edited by Carol Mighton Haddix

Surrey Books
Chicago

Design by Al Brandtner
Photographs copyright 2007 by Chris Cassidy. All rights reserved. Used with permission.

Printed in China.

Library of Congress Cataloging-in-Publication Data

Chicago cooks : 25 years of food history with menus, recipes, and tips from Les Dames d'Escoffier Chicago / Edited by Carol Mighton Haddix.
    p. cm.
  Summary: "A culinary history of Chicago's last 25 years told by the female chefs and food professionals who make up Les Dames d'Escoffier's Chicago chapter. Includes recipes and menus of regional specialties"-- Provided by publisher.
  Includes bibliographical references and index.
  ISBN-13: 978-1-57284-090-4 (hardback)
  ISBN-10: 1-57284-090-0 (hardback)
  1. Cookery. I. Mighton Haddix, Carol.

TX714.C468 2007
641.5--dc22

            2007016665

10 9 8 7 6 5 4 3 2

Surrey is an imprint of Agate Publishing. Agate books are available in bulk at discount prices. For more information, go to agatepublishing.com

TABLE OF CONTENTS

ACKNOWLEDGEMENTS

Thanks go to all the Chicago Les Dames d'Escoffier members who contributed their time, advice, recipes, stories and expertise to this book. And thanks to all the others (too numerous to mention) who have contributed to Chicago's amazing culinary story.

Also thanks to the Les Dames cookbook committee, which spent countless hours brainstorming ideas, titles, and menus and countless more hours writing, testing, editing, and proofing. The committee members are JeanMarie Brownson, Carol Mighton Haddix, Karen Levin, Sara Reddington, and Jill Van Cleave. Chapter president Barbara Glunz-Donovan spurred us on with encouragement and sound advice.

Additional recipe testers Dana Benigno, Maria Battaglia, Madelaine Bullwinkel, Lois Levine, Lisa Piasecki-Rosskamm, and Brenda McDowell made sure the recipes really worked. Pam Reardon ably spearheaded promotional efforts.

Kudos go to Dana Benigno, Joyce Lofstrom, and Diane Sokolofsky for their research and recipe introductions. Thanks also to historian Bruce Kraig for his advice and professorial grammar tips, and to Joan Reardon for her wise suggestions, indexing skills, and Les Dames member profiles.

Publisher Doug Seibold's vision for this book inspired us all. The editors and designers at Surrey Books fulfilled his and our hopes for this book with their talent and patience.

Photographer Chris Cassidy, prop-maestro Nancy Cassidy, food stylist Carol Smoler, and designer Queenie Burns turned our simple recipes into stunning photographs. Thanks. You made us so hungry!

FOREWORD

ON THE OCCASION OF OUR 25TH ANNIVERSARY, the members of Les Dames d'Escoffier Chicago offer this cookbook as both a commentary on Chicago's eclectic history of food and wine over the last 25 years and as an insight into our chapter.

Les Dames d'Escoffier Chicago is a group of women who have accepted challenges in various culinary professions; our ideas have caused people to listen, and our careers have opened new doors for other women. What better way to tell (and taste) our story—a story of a group of professional women with the simple yet dynamic mission to educate and support women in the culinary profession with events, seed money, and scholarships? What better way to celebrate than to take a closer look at both the organization and the city that has grown so much in culinary opportunities?

Our members include some of the city's most applauded restaurateurs and chefs, food journalists and cookbook authors, food stylists and recipe developers, food industry professionals and spokesmen, caterers and party planners, wine consultants, importers and retailers, and purveyors of fine products. Our workdays are dedicated to improving what we eat, what we drink, and how Chicagoans enjoy the whole concept of good living. Food, wine, and hospitality are our chosen fields, and by their very nature these professions become a lifestyle as much as a career.

As a group, we also recognize that many members of our community are in need, and we have given back to the community by sponsoring culinary scholarships, mentoring students, and providing funds to feed the hungry. Additionally, we have supported many projects that help women enter the professional culinary world.

By offering the recipes that we enjoy preparing for families and friends throughout the year, we invite you into our kitchens. Most of our menus reflect the real fact that we are "working women." Although time is scarce, we seek dishes that reflect our family traditions and are simple but delicious. The freshness and quality of the raw ingredients are of prime importance.

And what would a meal be without wine? Food and wine pairings are offered that will, we hope, enhance your meals.

This book is part history and part cookbook. Part One highlights Les Dames members' contributions to this city's thriving food scene. It also recognizes the many important culinary "characters" of the last 25 years who have helped put Chicago on the country's culinary stage. This is a history seen through Les Dames' eyes, so you'll find many of our names and our stories scattered throughout Part One. Recipes reflect the history of the city, so we've included some familiar Chicago classics, plus others from places and people who have contributed to our food heritage.

Part Two gathers together Les Dames members' favorite recipes, which we've grouped into 16 menus for entertaining throughout the year. Some of the recipes are for dishes we have served at Les Dames dinners, picnics and potlucks. Others are tried and true family treasures. All of these tested recipes give you a "taste" of Chicago, past and present.

This cookbook became a reality by virtue of the efforts of all of our members. The idea of a Les Dames cookbook began with a suggestion from Alma Lach, who published the monumental *Hows and Whys of French Cooking* in 1970. Since then, dozens of volumes by our members have been successfully published and enriched our city's culinary life.

Chicago, we present this cookbook to you as a gift for the hospitality you have shown us during the past 25 years. Our proceeds from the sales of this book will be donated to the Community Kitchens Program of The Greater Chicago Food Depository. This innovative program trains unemployed and underemployed people with the skills and ongoing support necessary to develop a successful career in the foodservice industry.

Les Dames d'Escoffier Chicago look forward to the next 25 years of sharing our professional lives, supporting each other, and sharing our expertise via career counseling and fundraising to provide for the needs of our community.

— Barbara Glunz
President, Les Dames d'Escoffier Chicago

WHO ARE THESE DAMES?

HOW DID A GROUP NICKNAMED "THE DAMES" (Les Dames is actually pronounced *lay dahm*) begin in Chicago?

In 1982, the late Elaine Sherman owned a cookware shop in Glenview called The Complete Cook. Sherman decided that there was a need in Chicago for a group geared to professional women in the food and/or wine business. Her idea solidified after a trip to New York City, where she learned about a new group founded by food journalist Carol Brock that was named after the French chef Auguste Escoffier: Les Dames d'Escoffier (LDE). Members of the group were professional women who were leaders in the fields of food, beverage, and hospitality. Brock borrowed the idea from a Boston confederation of the wives of members of a group called Les Amis d'Escoffier. A Washington, D.C. chapter of the new group was formed in 1981. Today, the Chicago chapter is one of the oldest and largest of 20-plus Les Dames chapters in the United States and Canada.

In early '80s Chicago, several other culinary groups existed. The dining organization Le Chaine de Rotisseurs, a group of food fanciers, held multicourse gourmet dinners in area restaurants and hotels, and the new American Institute of Wine and Food (begun by Julia Child and Robert Mondavi in 1981) was trying to get a Chicago chapter going. The Chicago Culinary Guild, a group of cooking teachers, food stylists, and others, had formed in 1979. There also were professional groups such as Home Economists in Business, the American Culinary Federation, the American Dietetic Association, and nutrition groups. The International Wine and Food Society had a Chicago chapter, and La Bonne Vie included leaders in the wine trade. But none were focused solely on professional women leaders across a broad range of culinary careers.

After she returned from her New York trip, Sherman gathered a group of 14 charter members who were inducted on May 23, 1982 at L'Escargot, a French restaurant on Michigan Avenue. Sherman chose women from a variety of food-industry occupations; the group included Jane Armstrong of Jewel Food Stores; Doris Banchet of Le Francais restaurant; Beverly Bennett, a food writer for the *Chicago Sun-Times*; Carolyn Buster of The Cottage restaurant; Jane Freiman, a cookbook author and teacher; Nancy Goldberg of Maxim's restaurant; Carol Mighton Haddix, food editor for the *Chicago Tribune*; Lucille Lampman of the Institute for Food and Family Living; Phyllis Magida, a food writer for the

WHO IS ESCOFFIER?

The namesake of Les Dames d'Escoffier was the most innovative chef in history, a man whose philosophy and accomplishments serve as both model and inspiration to culinary professionals today.

Auguste Escoffier began his long and distinguished professional culinary career in 1859 at the age of 13 and retired 61 years later. During his lifetime, he made French cuisine world famous. Escoffier also revolutionized and modernized menus, the practice of cooking, and the organization of the professional kitchen. Three of his cookbooks are still regarded as indispensable references.

Escoffier's prestige had the ripple effect of elevating the status of cooks from laborers to artists. Kaiser Wilhelm II once said to Escoffier, "I am the emperor of Germany, but you are the emperor of chefs."

Hotelier Cesar Ritz, who Escoffier met in 1890, provided not only the stage for the young chef's talents but also the audience. Escoffier headed Ritz's illustrious Savoy and Carlton hotels' kitchens in London during an era when the hotels' international clientele included most of the rich, powerful, and famous citizens of the world. The team of Ritz and Escoffier redefined restaurants and raised hospitality to unparalleled heights.

Escoffier's Le Guide Culinaire (1903) became "the primer for all cooks seeking to understand the complete repertoire of proper French cuisine," wrote David Kamp in The United States of Arugula. His rich dishes included lobster a la Americaine, poached Dover sole in Champagne sauce, and filet mignon with Bordelaise sauce. Chefs in the States and around the world soon were repeating and adapting his recipes.

Escoffier was also recognized by the French government, which made him a Chevalier of the Legion d'Honneur in 1920 and an officer of the Legion in 1928. His memoir, Memories of My Life, was translated into English in 1996, in celebration of the 150th anniversary of his birth.

Chicago Tribune; Leslee Reis of Café Provencal; Carole Segal of Crate & Barrel; Marian Tripp of Marian Tripp Communications; Nancy Versino, a wine consultant; and Jane Wallace of Restaurants & Institutions Magazine.

The group began meeting regularly at the Institute for Food and Family Living on Rush Street and worked excitedly to draw up bylaws and procedures with the advice and encouragement of Brock. With Sherman as its first president, Les Dames Chicago began planning the first of hundreds of programs to educate members and initiate networking opportunities that they believed were lacking in the Chicago culinary community.

Jill Van Cleave recalls working at the Institute of Food and Family Living during this period: "The first floor kitchen of this food-marketing firm was devoted to testing products and recipes for the Institute's clients—both foodservice and consumer product manufacturers. It was here that the first meetings of the Chicago chapter of Les Dames d'Escoffier took place at the invitation of the institute's director, Lucille Lampman. Lucille was a small woman with a strong, husky voice that she used to her advantage when managing her clients. The depth and breadth of her client list was impressive, and it provided fertile ground for acquiring the skills I needed to pursue my own career as a food consultant."

The charter Dames quickly identified other women to invite as members, and a second induction took place on Nov. 1, 1982 at Maxim's restaurant. Eighteen accomplished women joined the group as the "second wave." This second wave was chosen well, for from this new group would come four future presidents of Chicago Les Dames: Nancy Kirby Harris (1988-1992), Nancy Brussat Barocci (1992-1994), Abby Mandel (1994-1996), and Toria Emas (1996-1998). Each of the four later became president of Les Dames d'Escoffier International.

Membership grew each year to include a wide variety of professions—restaurateurs, chefs, wine professionals, journalists, authors, caterers, teachers, retailers, importers, public relations experts, photographers, and food stylists.

In those early years, Les Dames members found common ground in the programs they planned. There were seminars on chocolate, caviar, and sensory evaluation. There were cooking demonstrations, wine tastings, dim sum tastings, and visits with cookbook writers and national experts, such as winemaker Jill Davis, Anne Willan, and Alice Waters. There were summer potluck picnics with incredible arrays of food in Doris and Jean Banchet's Wheeling backyard. Jane Butel, a Southwest cuisine expert, taught members "How to Make a Perfect Margarita" in a session that some members were still talking about 25 years later! Members often met to share meals at many of Chicago's top restaurants, including Charlie Trotter's, Arun's, and Le Vichyssois.

Toria Emas, who began her career on the catering team at the Chicago Bar Association, rose to become Administration Director in charge of human resources, purchasing, telecommunications, and food services. Her administrative abilities would come in handy later, when she took on the role of president for the Chicago Les Dames chapter and, in 2006, as president of Les Dames d'Escoffier International.

CINNAMON BUNS

These cinnamon rolls are a part of The Chicago Bar Association's history. They predate the Great Depression and were considered a staple at the time. For many years, attorneys sat down to a lunch of two sweet rolls and a five-cent cup of coffee.

—*Toria Emas*

1 package (¼ ounce) active dry yeast	1 cup lukewarm milk
½ teaspoon sugar plus ½ cup granulated sugar	5 cups all-purpose flour
½ cup warm water (105-115°F)	2 tablespoons cinnamon sugar
½ cup (1 stick) butter, softened	1 cup (4 ounces) raisins
1 large egg	1 egg mixed with 1 tablespoon water
1 scant tablespoon salt	Confectioners' sugar

Dissolve the yeast and ½ teaspoon sugar in water in a small bowl. Let stand until bubbly, about 5 minutes. Beat the butter in the large bowl of an electric mixer with the flat paddle attachment until light and creamy. Beat in the ½ cup sugar until smooth. Beat in the egg, salt, and milk. Beat in 2 cups of the flour until smooth. Add the yeast mixture; continue to gradually beat in the remaining 3 cups flour to make a soft dough. Switch to the dough-hook attachment; mix on low speed 4 to 5 minutes until smooth and elastic. Place the dough in a generously buttered mixing bowl; cover with plastic wrap and let rise at room temperature until the dough doubles, about 2 hours.

Transfer the dough to a lightly floured work surface and divide in half. Roll half the dough out into a 14 x 8-inch rectangle. Sprinkle with half the cinnamon sugar and half the raisins. Starting at the short end, roll the dough up to enclose the filling. Cut into 6 rolls. Place the rolls on a nonstick baking sheet, cut side up and flattened slightly into a bun shape; space them evenly. Repeat with the remaining half of the dough. Cover loosely with cloth and let rise at room temperature for 30 minutes.

Preheat the oven to 375°F. Brush the buns with the egg mixture. Bake until golden brown, about 20 minutes. Transfer to a wire rack. Sprinkle liberally with sifted confectioners' sugar while still hot. Let cool to warm or room temperature before serving.

Makes 12 cinnamon rolls.

"During my term as Chicago chapter president, Les Dames d'Escoffier International celebrated the 150th anniversary of Auguste Escoffier's birth, and as coincidence would have it, I assumed the presidency of Les Dames International at the 160th anniversary of his birth," Emas said.

After four years as president, Sherman stepped down in 1986 and turned the gavel over to Carol Mighton Haddix, the *Tribune's* food editor, who often chaired meetings in the vintage walnut-paneled meeting rooms of Tribune Tower. Haddix and other chapter presidents met that same year in New York to unite the four existing chapters under the name Les Dames d'Escoffier International (LDEI), and Haddix served as vice president for the international group.

LES DAMES SERVE

As Les Dames Chicago grew, members began to fulfill the group's mission to help young people interested in culinary careers. They organized a scholarship fund benefit in 1986 at the Midland Hotel that featured a guided wine tasting by Italian wine expert Anthony Terlato of Paterno Wines. In June 1987 at the Ritz-Carlton Chicago, Nancy Kirby Harris chaired an elegant fundraising auction that would become an annual tradition in Chicago for many years and a forerunner of the city's many culinary benefits that are still so popular today. The first Food and Wine Auction drew hundreds of guests who sipped Champagne, nibbled appetizers from Les Dames chefs, and bid on exclusive auction items such as trips to Paris, meals at top restaurants, and cases of Bordeaux. That first event raised $26,000 for culinary scholarships.

The auction kept getting better each year. Les Dames scored a coup for the first auction of the 1990s (also held at the Ritz-Carlton) when Julia Child accepted its invitation to attend as honorary chairman. Earlier, Child had been honored with the title "Grande Dame" awarded by Les Dames d'Escoffier International. Although she also had been the Chicago auction's honorary chairman for several years, Child had never been able to attend due to scheduling conflicts. The *Tribune* reported that "the sight of the inimitable 6-foot-2 chef loping through the crowd brought an endless string of elbows jabbing ribs." The privilege of joining the famous cook for a "Breakfast with Julia" event the next day was up

for auction, which brought in a winning bid of $700. "There will NOT be oat bran," Child joked.

To promote the auction, members created a poster from an Eric Futran photograph featuring six of the city's top French chefs—Jean Banchet, Jean Joho, Gabino Sotelino, Pierre Pollin, Fernand Gutierrez, and Bernard Cretier. The posters sold out quickly. The auction, dedicated to the memory of founding Les Dames member Leslee Reis, who had recently passed away, raised $56,000 for the Greater Chicago Food Depository and CAREF (Cooking Advancement, Research and Education Foundation, for culinary scholarships).

As the auction's momentum grew during the next three years, the group raised thousands of dollars for culinary scholarships and for the food depository. Later, funds also went to the Inspiration Café, which provides meals and jobs for the homeless; to the C-Cap program, which trains public-school teachers and students in the culinary arts; and to Gallery 37, a city-sponsored culinary education program for high school students. Members also donated advice and hands-on help to the Flower Pot Café, a venture run by culinary students at Flower Vocational High School.

A TIME OF CHANGE
AND RENEWAL

By the mid-'90s, it was time to reflect on where the group had been, and where it was going. Then-president Abby Mandel, an author, teacher, and "The Weekend Cook" columnist for the *Chicago Tribune*, wrote in the chapter's newsletter: "Your board of directors has designated 1994-1995 as a time for reappraisal of and refocusing our chapter's activities and goals." A strategic-planning session produced a blueprint for the future that included an action plan and a new chapter mission statement: "To enhance our professional endeavors and to support each other through resource exchange, education, and community outreach." It was a time of change and renewal for the group. After hosting eight years of auctions at the Ritz-Carlton, the group decided to put the event on hold and instead voted to concentrate on smaller fundraising efforts devoted to creating an endowment for future fundraising goals.

For Escoffier's 150th birthday celebration, members orchestrated a magical six-course dinner in the style of the famous chef at the Ritz-Carlton Chicago. The fundraiser featured elegant French dishes prepared by Ritz chef Sarah Stegner and her staff and elegant service arranged by catering director Marlene Leone. Chairwomen Monique Hooker and Rose Kallas donned turn-of-the-century costumes to salute Escoffier in the proper style.

The annual summer picnics continued at members' homes until 1997, when Karen Levin organized the first of many annual potluck picnics at Ravinia. Levin served her famous margaritas (see recipe, page 152).

Members learned the ins and outs of making truffles in a master class taught by Madelaine Bullwinkel, and Sofia Solomon led a cheese seminar featuring French and American products paired with wines (see Planning the Cheese Course, page 152.

Fundraising took a more casual turn in 1999, when a benefit at Nacional 27 focused on Latin finger foods and Latin-inspired desserts created by chef Gale Gand.

DINNER WITH JULIA AT THE FLOWER POT CAFÉ

I vividly remember the evening Julia Child attended the grand opening dinner at the Flower Pot Café. With the help of Les Dames, Flower Vocational High School had developed a well-equipped teaching kitchen and launched a vending cart at the Garfield Park Conservatory, located across the street. The opening of the student-run Flower Pot Café was the school's most ambitious undertaking. For this occasion, Les Dames invited a celebrity guest— Julia Child.

A small regiment of awed waiters in new uniforms escorted Julia from the front door of the school to the kitchen. After meeting the teachers, she was led to a table and surrounded by student chefs in impeccable whites and toques. Several had prepared an imaginative pizza in her honor. After each one had made their presentation, Julia asked if they were planning to become chefs after graduation. Every last one of them said, "No!" Undaunted, Julia spoke briefly in her inimitably positive manner about the satisfaction of being a cook.

Dinner that night was served in a converted classroom on perfectly set linen-covered tables, including flower centerpieces. The quality of the meal and service were only exceeded by the sense of well-being we all shared after helping create such a successful program. Who knows? With Julia's help, we may have inspired someone to think seriously about a career in the food world.

—Madelaine Bullwinkel

HERB AND BEER GRILLED BARBECUE RIBS

Chef Carolyn Buster, a founding member of Les Dames d'Escoffier Chicago, and her husband Gerry located their restaurant, The Cottage, in the far south-suburban town of Calumet City. The Cottage put the town on the map for Chicago area diners looking for a fine meal. She wowed the crowd with these ribs at a Les Dames summer picnic at the home of Doris Banchet.

6	slabs baby back pork ribs (about 1¼ pounds each)
3	quarts water
2	onions, peeled and studded with whole cloves
4 to 5	cloves garlic, crushed
⅓	cup fresh *or* 2 tablespoons dried rosemary
2	tablespoons dried oregano
2	tablespoons crushed black peppercorns
1	tablespoon salt
1	tablespoon dried basil
2	teaspoons dried thyme
1	teaspoon dried marjoram
3	quarts beer
	Honey
4	cups Barbecue Sauce (recipe follows)

Choose a stockpot large enough to hold slabs of ribs (or cut ribs into pieces). Add the water, onions, garlic, and spices; heat to a boil. Add the beer, then add the ribs.

Cover and simmer until the ribs are tender and show no resistance when pierced with a fork, about 50 minutes. When tender, remove the ribs from the cooking liquid to baking sheets. Immediately brush the ribs generously on all sides with the honey; allow to cool. At this point, ribs may be stored, tightly covered, in the refrigerator for up to 3 days.

To finish, remove the ribs from the refrigerator while you build a charcoal fire or preheat a gas grill to medium heat. Grill the ribs in a single layer directly over medium-hot coals, turning frequently, until hot. Brush the ribs with the Barbecue Sauce, turning and coating each side at least twice, until browned. (Ribs will brown quickly, so watch them carefully.) Serve hot with extra sauce.

Makes 6 servings.

BARBECUE SAUCE

1	bottle (28 ounces) barbecue sauce
1	cup packed brown sugar
1	cup ketchup
¼	cup prepared mustard, hot or mild
½	cup fresh lemon juice
2	cloves garlic, crushed, *or* 1 teaspoon garlic powder
2	tablespoons crushed black peppercorns
½	tablespoon salt
	Few drops hot pepper sauce
½	teaspoon crushed dried red pepper (or more depending on taste)

Combine all the ingredients in a large saucepan. Heat to a boil. Remove from heat immediately and cool. Store covered in the refrigerator.

Makes 5 cups.

A 2001 Spring Market and Street Fair fundraiser—one of the first Chicago-area events designed to raise consciousness about the benefits of sustainable agriculture—connected vendors, farmers, and Les Dames chefs and members for a fun and chilly day outdoors. That same year, at a Derby Day brunch at the Cheney Mansion in Oak Park, Nancy Kirby Harris presented the chapter's first Dames of Distinction Award to Elaine Sherman. Harris called Sherman's contributions to the chapter—and to the community—"legendary." Sherman died a few weeks after being honored.

To celebrate its 20th year, the group gathered for another elegant auction at the Ritz with broadcaster and rancher Bill Kurtis as master of ceremonies. More than 100 items were up for bid to benefit charity and culinary scholarships. Among the buzz-worthy items were "Foodles," a batch of signed doodles of food or wine that were drawn by celebrities such as Chicago Mayor Richard M. Daley, Julia Child, Jacques Pepin, Alice Waters, and others.

In 2002, Marian Tripp, the founding member who ran her own food public-relations firm for 18 years and mentored many Les Dames members, received the second Dames of Distinction Award at the group's annual dinner, this time at Frontera Grill. Tripp died from complications from diabetes in 2004, and in that same year, Les Dames and the whole country mourned the loss of the Grande Dame, Julia Child, who passed away two days before her 92nd birthday. Julia had been a mentor and good friend to many members of Les Dames and other culinary groups.

In October 2004, Les Dames d'Escoffier International (LDEI) held its annual conference at Chicago's Knickerbocker Hotel; the conference's theme was "Sweet Home Chicago Is …" Members from around the country networked and attended seminars planned by the Chicago chapter: "The Art of Chocolate;" "Marketing Wines in the New Millennium;" "Urban Farmer's Markets: A Work in Progress;" and a "Midwestern Artisan Cheese Tasting." The conference's keynote speaker was Bill Kurtis, who addressed the importance of sustainable and organic crops.

In 2006, LDEI kicked off a new project called Green Tables, a civic agriculture and garden initiative to educate communities about the importance of fresh local produce. The Chicago chapter voted wholeheartedly to support the effort, including continuing to aid the city's only sustainable-food market, Green City Market.

"Escoffier, Dead or Alive?" was the provocative title of a 2006 Les Dames-sponsored panel discussion dealing with the legacy of the famed chef, author, and gastronomic visionary and his relevance to today's cuisine. Journalist William Rice moderated, leading panelists/chefs Graham Elliot Bowles of Avenues, Gale Gand of Tru, Jean Joho of Everest and Brasserie Jo, and Carrie Nahabedian of NAHA. Though food styles and kitchens have changed, the group concluded that much of what Escoffier taught remains ingrained in many restaurants, thus reaffirming his role in how America eats today.

Escoffier remains an appropriate namesake for "The Dames." The Chicago chapter continues his legacy of innovation, which is reflected in its members' many achievements and their role in Chicago's culinary growth. Les Dames International recognizes the chapter as a model for community involvement and leadership roles. Les Dames Chicago has dispersed more than $450,000 in culinary scholarships and grants to qualified women, educational facilities, and food banks.

Elaine Sherman's 1982 vision of a group of professional women who shared a commitment to the culinary arts remains vibrantly alive and ready to thrive in the great city of Chicago for another 25 years—and beyond.

PART ONE:

TWENTY-FIVE YEARS OF CHICAGO'S CULINARY ARTS

THE "CITY OF BIG SHOULDERS," as Carl Sandburg once dubbed Chicago, also could have easily been nicknamed the city of big appetites. The early residents of these swampy shores of Lake Michigan called the area Checagou, after the strong wild onions that grew abundantly in the region and were delicious in Native American stews. The tremendous growth of the city at the end of the 19th century was in no small part due to its location on the Great Lakes and close to the agricultural heartland of the country, which included bountiful wheat and corn crops and cattle-friendly plains to the south and west. Once railroads usurped steam ships for transporting these foodstuffs, Chicago's place in filling the nation's—and its own—growing appetites for food was secure. If the Midwestern and Plains states were the breadbaskets of America, then Chicago was the muscle-bound laborer who delivered the basket east of the Mississippi.

Providing food has always been central to Chicago. With such a historically significant background, is it any surprise that Chicago has risen to become one of the nation's culinary capitals? Tourists and business travelers come to Chicago in search of fine dining as well as its popular "street foods": deep-dish pizza, Italian-beef sandwiches, and the famous Chicago hot dog (forget the ketchup).

Many of the city's chefs are now considered world-class, winning accolades and awards from national organizations such as the James Beard Foundation and from the national press, including *Gourmet*, *Bon Appetit*, and *The New York Times*. Fine dining can be found in tiny chef-owned neighborhood restaurants, major hotels, and even in some of the city's chain restaurants. Where else could the Pump Room and the Parthenon, P.J. Grunts and Everest, Charlie Trotter's and Gold Coast Dogs co-exist and equally satisfy our tastes and appetites?

Chicago's neighborhoods brim with ethnic markets and immigrant-owned storefront restaurants. From Chinatown to Devon Avenue's Indian and Pakistani shops, and from Pilsen's Mexican eateries to Bronzeville's soul-food cafés, the streets are filled with aromas of delicious food.

The city's growing list of farmers' markets provides peak-season produce to more residents than ever before. Local supermarkets stock foods from around the world. More take-out prepared-food stores have opened in recent years, which provide busy families with another option for quick and delicious weeknight dinners.

There is no question—it's a fine time to be cooking and eating in Chicago.

DINING OUT IN CHICAGO

A CITY OF CHOICES

The network of restaurants in Chicago and its suburbs have seen amazing growth in their number and quality since the 1980s. With a few ups and down, the mostly robust economy helped fuel this growth. The increasing sophistication of diners, from well-traveled Chicagoans to visiting conventioneers, has supported restaurants that offer top-quality food and service. As Sylvia Lovegren, author of *Fashionable Food: Seven Decades of Food Fads*, wrote, the rising numbers of double-income families meant more were opting to eat out, and restaurants increasingly became a solution to a nagging question: "What's for

dinner?" As time wore on, fewer people had time for or the inclination to cook from scratch at home.

In the 1980s, Chicago's hot-dog stands and classic steakhouses, such as Gene & Georgetti's and Eli Shulman's popular Eli's: The Place for Steak, continued to attract red-meat lovers. Classic Chicago restaurants such as The Berghoff, Crickets, Jacques, Lou Mitchell's, the Cape Cod Room, and Arnie's all enjoyed brisk business. Don Roth's Blackhawk featured its famous spinning salad, a 21-item dish prepared tableside in a bowl spun on a bed of ice. Louis Szathmary's The Bakery had been going strong with the famous chef's Continental menu (featuring such

CHICAGO CLASSICS

Chicago's versions of "street food" are heartier than most—there are no dainty items, like the satay sticks of Indonesia, dumplings of China, or tacos of Mexico. We go for hot dogs heaped with condiments, pizzas layered deep in a two-inch high pan, or big sandwich rolls stuffed and dripping with slices of beef and hot peppers. It's food for the really hungry: Chicago hot dogs, deep-dish and stuffed pizzas, and Italian beef sandwiches.

Of course, there are also the restaurant dishes created here that have come to symbolize Chicago through the years—shrimp de Jonghe, chicken Vesuvio, Greek gyros, Eli's Cheesecake, and, of course, the great steaks that have made Chicago famous since the days of the stockyards. *—Carol Mighton Haddix*

CHICKEN VESUVIO

We're not sure who invented chicken Vesuvio, but it was no doubt born in one of this town's great mom-and-pop Italian restaurants as a version of some southern Italian chicken dish. This recipe is adapted from the Ethnic Chicago Cookbook, *which was edited by Chicago Tribune food editor Carol Mighton Haddix.*

⅓ cup all-purpose flour	1 broiler/fryer chicken, about 3 pounds, cut up
1½ teaspoons dried basil	½ cup olive oil
¾ teaspoon dried leaf oregano	3 baking potatoes, cut into lengthwise wedges
½ teaspoon salt	
¼ teaspoon each dried leaf thyme	3 tablespoons chopped fresh parsley
¼ teaspoon freshly ground pepper	3 cloves garlic, minced
Pinch dried rosemary	¾ cup dry white wine
Pinch dried rubbed sage	

Mix the flour, basil, oregano, salt, thyme, pepper, rosemary, and sage in shallow dish. Dredge the chicken in the flour mixture; shake off excess.

Heat the oil in a 12-inch cast-iron or other ovenproof skillet over medium-high heat until hot. Add the chicken pieces in a single layer. Cook, turning occasionally, until browned on all sides, about 15 minutes. Remove with tongs to paper towels.

Heat the oven to 375°F. Add the potato wedges to the skillet. Fry, turning occasionally, until light brown on all sides, about 10 minutes. Remove to the paper towels.

Pour off all but 2 tablespoons of the oil from the skillet. Return the chicken and potatoes to the skillet. Sprinkle with parsley and garlic; pour wine over the mixture. Cover and bake for 10 minutes. Uncover; bake until the potatoes are fork-tender and the thigh juices run clear, about 15 to 20 minutes. Let stand 5 minutes before serving. Serve with the pan juices.

Makes 4 servings.

delights as duck liver pâté and beef Wellington) for about 20 years.

THE RISE OF NOUVELLE CUISINE

But a new French style of cooking called nouvelle cuisine began to get all the press. The trend was nicely described by David Leite on his website, *Leite's Culinaria*: "Diners paid significantly more to eat significantly less, and loved it." Nouvelle cuisine's lighter sauces and smaller portions, which were first introduced by a small band of young chefs in France, soon made their way to many of America's fine dining restaurants.

Many Chicago chefs toyed with the nouvelle cuisine concepts, including two top restaurateurs—Jean Banchet and Jovan Trboyevic.

Trboyevic's Le Perroquet on Walton Street was often cited as one of the best restaurants in town. At Le Perroquet, customers could expect stellar service and refined dishes, including its famous soufflés. In fact, Trboyevic was the first in Chicago to offer an oh-so-nouvelle fruit, kiwi.

At Le Francais, in northwest suburban Wheeling, Banchet ran the kitchen, and his wife, Doris, skillfully supervised the front of the restaurant. The Banchets attracted customers from the city 45 minutes away and also brought in diners from all over the country. "Expensive ingredients exquisitely and imaginatively prepared," raved the 1979 edition of *Where to Eat in America*, edited by Burton Wolf and William Rice, "but be prepared to spend 2½ to 3 hours and at least $40 per person."

Carrie Nahabedian, chef/owner of Clark Street's NAHA, worked with Jean Banchet early in her career. She remembers Le Francais as definitely *not* in the school of "less is more." "It was the temple of American gastronomy, and people *dined*—they did not *eat*," she said. She remembers Banchet saying, "No cost is too great. Always buy the best that you can afford. People will remember."

Many of the tenets of nouvelle cuisine would continue to influence chefs and would eventually lead to a new style of American cooking. Arlington Heights' Le Titi de Paris, which chef Pierre Pollin purchased in 1978 and ran successfully until his 2006 retirement, also featured the new French fare (such as a sausage of spinach noodles, seafood mousse and vinegar basil butter sauce).

Carlos' opened in 1981 in a Highland Park space that had been formerly occupied by a grocery store. At Carlos', Carlos and Debbie Nieto offered a nouvelle French menu that added Asian influences (such as soft-shelled crab with jasmine tea sauce). The chef was Roland Liccioni, formerly of Alouette, who worked side-by-side with his wife, pastry chef Mary Beth Liccioni. A succession of chefs followed the Liccionis at Carlos', and many went on to open or run their own fine-dining kitchens.

TRADITIONAL FRENCH FARE SURVIVES

Despite the rise of nouvelle cuisine, traditional French cooking held strong in Chicago. Maxim's de Paris, owned by the confirmed Francophile Nancy Goldberg, recreated the elegant Art Nouveau décor and Escoffier-like dishes of the famed Paris institution on Chicago's Gold Coast. Goldberg loved

CHICAGO-STYLE ITALIAN BEEF SANDWICHES

Beef stands have sprung up in many neighborhoods; most locals have their favorite. This Chicago Tribune *recipe makes it easy to make your own. Don't forget to offer both hot and sweet peppers.*

- 1 teaspoon crushed red pepper
- 1 teaspoon garlic powder
- 1 teaspoon dried basil
- 1 teaspoon dried oregano
- 1 teaspoon freshly ground black pepper
- ½ teaspoon salt
- 1 small sirloin tip roast, about 2½ pounds
- 1 cup cold water
- 8 soft or hard Italian rolls, warmed, split
   Pickled hot sport peppers for serving
   Sautéed sweet bell peppers, sliced

Preheat the oven to 450°F. Combine the seasonings; rub ½ of the mixture over the meat, including some under the fat layer. Put the meat into a shallow pan just large enough to hold it. Roast for 15 minutes, then reduce the temperature to 350°F. Continue to cook 20 minutes longer.

Remove from the oven; pour cold water and the remaining seasoning mixture into the pan. Return to the oven; cook until the meat registers 135°F, about 20 minutes. Remove from the pan; cool 20 minutes. (Temperature will continue to rise, reaching 145°F for medium-rare.)

Meanwhile, degrease the pan juices and transfer to a saucepan; cook over medium heat until heated through, about 3 minutes. Slice the meat into paper-thin slices. For each sandwich, dip meat slices briefly into juice. Layer meat and juices into a warmed, split roll. Serve immediately topped with peppers as desired.

Makes 8 servings.

SHRIMP DE JONGHE

This simple recipe is a close approximation of the original dish, which was created at Monroe Street's De Jonghe Hotel either by the hotel's owner, Henri de Jonghe, or his chef, Emil Zehr. The hotel was shuttered during Prohibition for serving liquor. This recipe is adapted from the Chicago Tribune.

- 1½ quarts water
- ½ small onion, sliced
- 1 rib celery, halved
- 3 black peppercorns
- 1 bay leaf
- ¼ teaspoon salt
- 1½ pounds large raw shrimp in the shell
- ½ cup (1 stick) unsalted butter, melted, divided
- 2 tablespoons dry sherry or white wine
- 1½ cups coarse French bread crumbs
- 2 tablespoons minced fresh parsley
- 1 tablespoon minced shallot
- 2 cloves garlic, minced
- ½ teaspoon sweet paprika
- ⅛ teaspoon ground red pepper (cayenne)

Heat the water, onion, celery, peppercorns, bay leaf, and salt to a boil in a large saucepan over medium-high heat. Add the shrimp; cover. Return to a boil; drain. Run the shrimp under cold water to cool. Peel the shrimp; transfer to a large bowl. Add half of the melted butter and the sherry; toss to mix.

Preheat the oven to 400°F. Combine the remaining melted butter, bread crumbs, parsley, shallot, garlic, paprika, and red pepper in a small bowl. Spoon half of the shrimp mixture into a buttered 1½ quart baking dish. Top with ½ of the bread crumbs. Top with the remaining shrimp mixture, then the remaining bread crumbs. Bake until the crumbs are lightly browned, about 10 minutes.

Makes 4 servings.

ONION FLAN

My husband, Bernard, created this flan for the annual Shriner's Vidalia Onion Sale. Our customers at
Le Vichyssoise enjoy it with tender fingerling potatoes and a fresh chive vinaigrette.
When Vidalia onions are not available, any mild, sweet onion can be substituted. — Priscilla Cretier

2	sliced sweet onions, such as Vidalia (about 4 ounces each)
2	tablespoons unsalted butter
	Salt and pepper, to taste
1	egg
½	cup heavy (whipping) cream
4	fingerling potatoes, cooked and peeled

CHIVE VINAIGRETTE DRESSING:

2	tablespoons extra virgin olive oil
1	tablespoon white or red wine vinegar
1	tablespoon demi-glace (such as Natural Classics brand)
1	teaspoon chopped chives
	Salt and pepper, to taste

Preheat the oven to 425 degrees. Butter 4 nonstick 4-inch tart pans. Set the pans on a baking sheet. Cook the sliced onions in butter in a large skillet over low heat, stirring occasionally, until tender but not browned, about 10 minutes. Season to taste with salt and pepper; drain off butter.

Placed the cooked onions over the bottoms of the buttered tart pans (about ¾ of the pan should be covered with onion). Mix the egg and cream together in a small bowl; season to taste with salt and pepper. Pour over the onions and stir to blend together. Bake until golden brown, about 15 minutes. Let stand in a warm place 10 minutes.

Meanwhile, for dressing, whisk all ingredients in a medium bowl until smooth. Unmold the onion flan onto a plate; cut the fingerling potatoes in half lengthwise and place 2 halves on each plate. Drizzle dressing on the potatoes and around the flan.

Makes 4 first-course servings.

French food and, especially, French wine. Toria Emas, now president of Les Dames International, recalls one early Les Dames event held at Maxim's, in which the group brought in its own wines. Unfortunately, they were planning to serve a California sparkling wine. Goldberg would have none of that.

"She replaced our wine with true Champagne," recalled Emas. "Her drink of choice was Krug."

Bernard Cretier was Maxim's chef during its most prominent years, but in 1976, he and wife Priscilla relocated to McHenry County to open a country French restaurant, Le Vichyssois. Bernard's great hand with dishes such as onion flan, seafood pate with tomato and basil sauce, bouillabaisse and cassoulet drew diners north from the city to celebrate many special occasions.

After Cretier's departure, Goldberg leased the restaurant to George Badonsky, who brought in a young Alsatian chef, Jean Joho. Joho's nuanced French dishes quickly earned raves from the *Tribune* and *Sun-Times*. However, Goldberg decided to close the restaurant in 1982, and Joho moved on to join

Chicago restaurateur extraordinare Richard Melman in other restaurant projects. Today, Maxim's still looks the same, but it is owned by the city of Chicago and is exclusively used for special events; today, it is called Maxim's: The Nancy Goldberg International Center.

Fernand Gutierrez, a native of Dijon, France, brought his classical French food training to the Ritz-Carlton's Dining Room. Carrie Nahabedian remembers, "Fernand Gutierrez was my mentor. He used to say, 'Be true to the discipline that sets the bar for excellence, and never forget that it's all about the people. Don't ever compromise. Cook each dish as if you were the guest.'"

A more informal French favorite was Evanston's Café Provençal, which opened in 1977. The "French-provincial setting" featured "some of the best country-French cooking in the area," according to *Where to Eat in America*. Owner Leslee Reis, a founding member of Les Dames, cooked up seasonal menus with dishes such as cassoulet, chicken with morels in Madeira sauce, salmon with fresh-basil sauce, and apple tartlets. The combination of flavorful food, professional service, and Reis's personal style brought customers from all over the Chicago area and around the country. Reis died in 1990, after many years of awards and recognition for Café Provençal.

THE MOVE TO AMERICAN FARE

Nouvelle cuisine continued to influence Chicago's chefs, but many began to experiment with regional ingredients. In *Fashionable Food*, Lovegren noted that chefs in Chicago and elsewhere were influenced by other trends during the '80s that guided a new

APPLE TARTLETS

Leslee Reis, my good friend and the talented owner of Evanston's Café Provençal, shared this recipe with me. Simple ingredients are transformed into a dessert of unmatched perfection. The tartlets are best served warm, but they can be assembled in advance and held in the refrigerator. The only last-minute work is the baking.

— Abby Mandel

½	of a package of (17.3 ounces) frozen puff pastry, thawed
2	medium Granny Smith or Jonathon apples (about 12 ounces), cored, peeled, halved lengthwise, thinly sliced
2	tablespoons sugar
½	teaspoon ground cinnamon
1	tablespoon unsalted butter, cut into pea-size pieces
	Vanilla ice cream and warm caramel sauce, for serving

Preheat the oven to 450°F. Place the rack in the center of the oven; have a large baking sheet ready. On a floured board, roll out the puff pastry as thinly as possible, to ¹/₁₆-inch thickness. Cut four 6-inch circles of dough. Carefully transfer to a baking sheet and place in the freezer for 10 minutes.

Arrange the apple slices in a circle of tight petals on each pastry round. Combine the sugar and cinnamon and sprinkle it over the apples; dot with butter. Refrigerate until ready to bake. This can be prepared up to 6 hours in advance.

Bake until golden and the apples are tender, about 15 minutes. Serve immediately, topped with ice cream and drizzled with caramel sauce.

Makes 4 servings.

CHOCOLATE TOWN

The 1980s could be termed our town's chocolate decade. Chicago, of course, has always been a candy town. From the first Mars bars to Fannie May, Blommer's, Dove Bars, and Frango Mints, the city has embraced chocolate manufacturers. Chicago quickly became known as the candy capital of the U.S.

In restaurants, tiramisu and chocolate cakes hit the dessert carts in a big way in the 1980s. In Chicago and throughout the nation, we downed chocolate decadence cakes, truffles, and white chocolate mousse with abandon. In the '90s, chocolate continued its run, with individual "molten" cakes with liquid chocolate centers and infused chocolates featuring exotic flavors, such as tea, curry, red pepper, passion fruit, and Champagne.

Chocolate "lounges" appeared in the early 2000s, and chocolate industry giants like Ghirardelli and Hershey's opened shops on and near the Magnificent Mile. Artisan chocolatiers opened shops all over town; some learned the craft at The French Pastry Institute, a top-notch school in the Loop. Vosges and Coco Rouge are just two of the latest chocolatiers enjoying success—sweet news for Chicagoans, indeed. —*Carol Mighton Haddix*

CHOCOLATE SOUFFLÉ CAKE

When I first discovered the new genre of "flourless" chocolate cakes in the 1980s, they were all deep, dark, and dense. I wondered if the cake could go "butterless" as well! This turned out to be my all-time favorite, and when my former husband, Capt. Bill Pinkney, returned from his solo sail around the world, he told me that it was the only dessert he had longed for and asked me to make it on his first day home. — *Ina Pinkney*

CAKE:

- 9 large eggs, separated, at room temperature
- 1 cup confectioners' sugar
- ½ cup unsweetened cocoa powder
- 1 teaspoon vanilla extract
- ½ teaspoon cream of tartar

FROSTING:

- 4 cups cold heavy (whipping) cream
- ½ cup confectioners' sugar
- ¼ cup unsweetened cocoa powder
- White or dark chocolate shavings, for garnish

Preheat the oven to 350°F. Line the bottom of a 9-inch springform pan with parchment paper. Butter or oil sides of pan. For the cake, combine the egg yolks, confectioners' sugar, and cocoa powder in a medium bowl. Beat until thick and lightened in color. Stir in the vanilla; set aside.

Beat the egg whites in a large, clean mixing bowl until frothy; large bubbles should appear around the edge. Add the cream of tartar and increase the mixing speed until the whites are thick and glossy. (To test, tilt the bowl. If the whites slide, they need a little more beating.) Gently fold a large spoonful of the beaten whites into the chocolate mixture to lighten it. Gently fold the remaining whites and the chocolate mixture together. Carefully spoon into the prepared pan.

Bake 35 to 40 minutes. The cake will be rounded when removed from the oven, and the center will sink as it cools. Cool completely on a wire rack; remove from the pan by carefully loosening the edges with a metal spatula.

For the frosting, combine the cream, confectioners' sugar, and cocoa powder in a chilled bowl. Beat with chilled beaters, with the electric mixer set at low speed. Scrape the bowl; increase the speed and beat until the beaters leave a definite imprint in the whipped cream. Spread the filling smoothly over the top and sides of the cooled cake. Garnish with white or dark chocolate shavings or sprinkles. Keep refrigerated until ready to serve.

Makes 10 to 12 servings.

FLOURLESS CHOCOLATE CAKE

This recipe proved to be a 23-year favorite at Gordon Sinclair's restaurant Gordon. The dapper Sinclair was among the first 10 restaurateurs in America named by Cook's Magazine *as having contributed the most to American cuisine. (Today, these awards are known as the James Beard Awards.) This now-classic cake is always a winner.*

7	tablespoons unsalted butter, divided
9	ounces semi-sweet high-quality chocolate (such as Valrhona or Scharffen Berger), chopped into small pieces
7	large eggs, separated, at room temperature
	Pinch of salt
⅓	cup granulated sugar
	Whipped cream, for serving

Preheat the oven to 250°F. Generously coat an 8 x 2-inch round cake pan with 1 tablespoon butter. Dust the bottom of the pan with flour; refrigerate until needed. Melt the chocolate and the remaining 6 tablespoons of the butter in a double boiler set over simmering water (or melt in a microwave oven on medium or 50% power until nearly melted, 2 to 3 minutes, and then stir until completely melted).

Beat the egg yolks lightly in a small bowl; stir a small amount of chocolate into the yolks. Then, beat the yolk mixture into the remaining melted chocolate until blended. Set aside.

Beat the egg whites with a pinch of salt in the large bowl of an electric mixer at medium speed until the whites just begin to stiffen. Gradually add the sugar, beating until the whites are stiff, but not dry. Stir a small amount of egg whites into the chocolate to lighten it. Then, use a large rubber spatula to thoroughly fold the chocolate mixture into the egg whites. Spoon into the prepared cake pan. Place the cake pan on a baking sheet.

Bake until the center is set but jiggles slightly, 40 to 45 minutes. Remove from the oven to a wire rack. Cool 15 minutes, then invert the cake onto a serving plate and remove the pan. Let cool to room temperature. Serve with freshly whipped cream.

Makes 10 to 12 servings.

Note

The cake can't be tested with a knife, and the baked cake should not be stored in the refrigerator. It may be kept, covered, at room temperature for 1 day.

CHOCOLATE PECAN CARAMEL TORTE

The late Elaine Sherman, founder of Les Dames Chicago and known as Madame Chocolate by her colleagues, used her culinary skills to teach cooking in people's homes and to introduce them to fine chocolates and quality cookware. This recipe is adapted from her 1984 cookbook, Madame Chocolate's Book of Divine Indulgences. *A quote from Elaine typifies her devotion to this ingredient: "Chocolate is heavenly, mellow, sensual, deep, dark, sumptuous, gratifying, potent, dense, creamy, seductive, suggestive, rich, excessive, silky, smooth, luxurious, celestial. Chocolate is downfall, happiness, pleasure, love, ecstasy, fantasy ... chocolate makes us wicked, guilty, sinful, healthy, chic, happy."*

CRUST:

- 8½ ounces chocolate wafer cookies
- 2 tablespoons granulated sugar
- 4 tablespoons unsalted butter, melted

CHOCOLATE MOUSSE:

- 1 package (16 ounces) bittersweet or semi-sweet chocolate chips
- 4 large egg yolks
- 6 tablespoons strong brewed coffee
- 1 cup (2 sticks) unsalted butter, cut into pieces

- ½ cup granulated sugar
- 6 large egg whites
- 4 teaspoons warm water

PECAN-CARAMEL LAYER:

- 2 cups (8 ounces) pecans, coarsely chopped
- 2 cups packed light brown sugar
- 1 cup (2 sticks) unsalted butter
  Pinch salt
- ½ to ⅔ cup heavy (whipping) cream, divided
- 1½ cups (6 ounces) pecan halves

For the crust, preheat the oven to 350°F. Line the bottom of a 10-inch springform pan with foil; spray the pan with vegetable cooking spray. Process the wafer cookies and sugar in a food processor to fine crumbs. With the machine running, drizzle melted butter through the food tube. Scrape the sides of the bowl and process an additional 5 seconds. Place the crumb mixture in the bottom of the prepared pan and spread into an even layer. Chill 5 minutes and then bake 5 minutes. Cool completely on a wire rack.

For the chocolate mousse, place half of the chocolate into the dry bowl of a food processor. With the machine running, add the remaining chocolate through the food tube and process until the chocolate is ground to small beads. Add the egg yolks and process 5 seconds or until blended. Heat the coffee, butter, and sugar in a small saucepan until the sugar is dissolved and the mixture is simmering. With the processor running, pour the hot coffee mixture through the food tube. Stop the machine to scrape the sides and process until smooth. Transfer the mixture to a large mixing bowl. Combine the egg whites and water in bowl of electric mixer. Beat on medium-high speed until the whites are whipped to firm peaks. With a large spatula, fold the egg whites into the chocolate mixture and refrigerate until almost set, about 30 minutes.

For the pecan-caramel layer, put the chopped pecans into a bowl. Heat the brown sugar, butter, and salt in a small heavy saucepan until the sugar dissolves. Add ½ cup of the cream. Heat to boil and simmer until the caramel thickens enough to coat the back of spoon, 1 to 2 minutes. Pour half of the caramel over the chopped pecans; mix and then immediately pour over the crumb crust. Refrigerate until the caramel sets. (Reserve the remaining caramel in the saucepan.)

Spoon the chocolate mousse over the caramel layer; smooth the top. Refrigerate for several hours, until firmly set.

To finish, arrange the pecan halves in a decorative pattern over the top of the mousse. Reheat the reserved caramel over low heat, adding the remaining cream to thin, if necessary. Cool the caramel slightly, then pour evenly on top. (Use a pastry brush, if necessary, to spread the caramel.) Refrigerate until firm, at least 2 hours.

Remove the cake from the pan and place on a serving dish. To serve, cut with a hot knife.

Makes 14 to 16 servings.

Note:
Torte freezes beautifully, well wrapped. Defrost overnight in the refrigerator.

---

movement that emphasized American food. So-called California cuisine, popularized at institutions such as Alice Waters' Chez Panisse in Berkeley, California, gained notice. Next came the Cajun cuisine boom, which made stars of New Orleans-based chefs such as Paul Prudhomme, of K-Paul's Louisiana Kitchen, and Emeril Lagasse, who cooked up "new" New Orleans cuisine at Commander's Palace. Upscale Southwest cuisine also gained momentum through the decade, and chilies burned their way into our culinary consciousness.

As chefs such as New York's Larry Forgione and California's Jeremiah Tower hyped their styles of American food in the early '80s, Chicago restaurateurs Gordon Sinclair, Carolyn Buster, and Michael Foley served their own versions, which featured fresh ingredients and light sauces that were based on French techniques but featured American inventiveness.

In 1974, Buster, a founding member of Les Dames, and her husband Gerry opened a charming restaurant, The Cottage, in an unlikely location—the far south-suburban town of Calumet City. The locale drew few visitors by itself, but The Cottage put the town on the map for Chicago-area diners looking for a fine meal. Buster's style of cooking was grounded in classical methods, and her menu showed spectacular range, including a Continental-style pork schnitzel, seafood ravioli with anchovy butter sauce, and her signature raspberry cake. One memorable all-garlic dinner showcased Buster's talents well, including a surprisingly good garlic ice cream.

Two years later, Sinclair opened his pioneering Gordon restaurant on then-seedy Clark Street. Despite the state of the neighborhood, city diners and suburbanites flocked to Gordon. Sinclair and chef John Terczak became widely known for clever dishes like artichoke fritters Béarnaise, and they are considered to have "invented" the flourless chocolate cake, a rich, almost fudge-like cake that would soon be found on menus all over town. The restaurant moved down the block in 1982 and closed on New Year's Eve of 1999, but over the years Sinclair received many accolades for his contributions to American cuisine.

Michael Foley was one of the first chefs in Chicago to embrace the use of Midwestern ingredients in

American dishes. In 1981, he opened Printer's Row restaurant in the neighborhood of the same name. With a menu that changed weekly, Foley experimented with innovative dishes such as grilled salmon in pink peppercorn sauce, duckling with corn crepes, or wild mushrooms with pine needles. Restaurant critic Sherman Kaplan noted that Printer's Row "was the best thing to happen to the South Loop since paved streets and street lamps."

Elsewhere in the city, restaurant entrepreneur Richard Melman had been opening a string of fun, themed restaurants throughout the '70s with his firm, Lettuce Entertain You Enterprises. But in 1976, he moved into the fine-dining arena by taking over the famous Pump Room restaurant and upgrading its somewhat tired menu. In 1980, Melman and chef Gabino Sotelino opened Lincoln Park's Ambria, which featured a modern French-influenced menu. After Ambria proved to be a success, he gambled on a few more—a modern Italian spot, Avanzare, and, later in the decade, the French high-rise Everest, with Jean Joho as chef. A tapas place, Café Ba-Ba-Reeba, which was another partnership with Sotelino, was a big hit, and Shaw's Crab House was Melman's ode to the seafood houses of the 1940s. Shaw's dining room boasts an "Oyster Hall of Fame," which honors famous oystermen, purveyors, and writers including Joan Reardon, author of *Oysters*.

Another Chicago institution is the Levy Restaurant Group, which moved into the fine-dining arena with the debut of its high-end Italian restaurant, Spiaggia, on Michigan Avenue. When the restaurant opened, Tony Mantuano was its chef, and Suzanne Florek served as his assistant chef.

When Mantuano left to open the more casual Tuttoposto in River North, Florek joined him there. Later, Mantuano returned to Spiaggia, where he remains to this day.

CHICAGO'S OWN CELEBRITY CHEFS

Chicago's rise to national culinary prominence gained a double boost in 1987. That year, Charlie Trotter and Rick and Deann Bayless opened restaurants that brought the city the acclaim of the foodie elite. The Baylesses, who were confirmed Mexican aficionados, had been working on a Mexican cookbook after spending years traveling throughout that country, and they decided to open an authentic Mexican restaurant that featured the foods they had been sampling for years. Clark Street's Frontera Grill was the result, and soon lines of customers waited in front of the no-reservation restaurant. Word spread well beyond Chicago, and a few years later, the Baylesses opened a fancier restaurant next door called Topolobampo.

"We thought Chicago was a wonderful city," Deann Bayless explained. "We could get the Mexican ingredients we needed and the choice here was much better than L.A., where we considered opening, too. Chicago at the time was dominated by Lettuce Entertain You and the Levy brothers. We had to compete with them. Their restaurants didn't take reservations, and had moderate prices. There were very few chef-owned restaurants back then. We knew we had to give something that Lettuce and Levy couldn't, and that was the personal input.

"We were busy from the start," she said. "Our

CEVICHE SALAD WITH AVOCADO, CILANTRO AND GREEN CHILIES

For centuries in Mexico, ceviche has meant ultra-fresh fish or shellfish that's marinated or "acid-cooked" in fresh lime juice. My version here is traditionally Mexican, except that the fish in Mexico would often be mackerel or kingfish, and it would typically be marinated long enough to "cook" through. I've recently become enchanted with the Peruvian take on ceviche (the fish is marinated only moments before serving), especially since sashimi-grade fish (the top, okay-to-eat-raw grade) is becoming more common in our fish markets. Whatever your marinating preference, this salad is just the ticket on a warm summer night, served with crusty bread or crackers.

—*Deann Bayless*

This recipe was originally published in *Mexican Everyday* (W. W. Norton).

1   cup fresh lime juice
2   cloves garlic, coarsely chopped
1   cup loosely packed cilantro, coarsely chopped
    Fresh hot green chilies to taste, stemmed and coarsely chopped (such as 2 serranos or 1 jalapeño)
1   teaspoon salt *or* to taste
1   to 1¼ pounds sashimi-grade boneless skinless fish (such as tuna, snapper or salmon), cut into ½-inch cubes, *or* about 1 to 1¼ pounds medium to small cooked shrimp
1   ripe avocado, peeled, pitted, and cut into ¼-inch cubes
1   large head of Boston, or butterhead, lettuce, leaves separated
1   green onion, thinly sliced, for garnish

In a blender or food processor, combine the lime juice, garlic, cilantro, chilies, and salt. Process until smooth.

Scoop the fish into a large bowl. Pour the lime marinade over, stirring to coat all the surfaces. Let stand and "cook" in the lime juice to suit your own taste: you can eat it right away (Peruvian-style) if you like raw fish, or let it "cook" for an hour or two if you like it more well-done; cooked shrimp needs only a few minutes to soak up the flavor. It takes about 4 hours to "cook" the fish to well-done in lime juice; if that is your desire, add the cilantro just before serving to preserve its fresh color.

Pour off half of the marinating liquid; set aside. Toss the avocado with the fish, then taste and season with additional salt if necessary.

Divide the lettuce between 4 dinner plates. Scoop a portion of the ceviche into the center of each plate. Sprinkle with the chopped green onion. To serve, drizzle some reserved lime marinade over the lettuce.

Makes 4 servings.

Mexican cookbook came out on the same day we opened, so we seemed to explode on the scene. We had a quote from Craig Claiborne of the *New York Times* on the back of the book ... he liked it. So his colleague, Marian Burros, was in our restaurant within the first two months and wrote about us in the *Times*. That certainly helped vault us. One of the most satisfying things in Chicago is seeing how many more chef-owned restaurants there are now. This city has never let us down."

Trotter, on the other hand, was creating a different style of cuisine that was all his own. After training in Europe and elsewhere in the States, Trotter came on the scene—ready for culinary battle—while still in his 20s. Charlie Trotter's opened in a Lincoln Park townhouse and wowed the critics from the get-go with his imaginative combinations of fresh and often unusual ingredients. With impeccable service and an extensive wine list managed by great sommeliers, such as Larry Stone, Joe Spellman, and Belinda Chang, Charlie Trotter's has drawn crowds from the very start, and Trotter has commanded a place on the culinary must-visit list of chefs and food lovers around the country.

THE '90S AND BEYOND

Chicago's appetite for dining out has steadily grown. The Taste of Chicago, a summertime outdoor food festival, has reflected the growing popularity of restaurants. By the late '80s, the Taste had morphed from its beginnings as a musical festival with some food booths on Navy Pier to the premier food event for the city. Thanks in large part to the efforts of restaurateur Arnie Morton, the Taste moved first to Michigan Avenue and then on to Grant Park, expanding more and more each summer. Today, the Taste includes more than 60 restaurants that sell samples of their specialties. It remains the city's most popular festival, bringing in crowds every summer from around the Midwest.

Through the ups and downs of the economy in the 1990s, Chicagoans continued to enjoy the city's vibrant restaurant scene. By 1993, according to James Traeger's *The Food Chronology*, Americans spent almost 30 percent of their food dollars on restaurant meals, a significant increase from 22 percent in 1978. They spent only 51 percent of these dollars in food stores, which was a decrease from 59 percent.

Eating out meant an "experience." Restaurants were theater; décor, ambience, food, and service combined to create an evening of entertainment. One popular Rush Street spot, Yvette's, brought in jazz performers. Kitchens were opened to the dining room, so diners could see the chefs in action. Chefs became stars. As chefs moved from restaurant to restaurant, their fans followed. "Foodies" awaited the openings of new restaurants like teenage fans of rock stars.

It was the time of the "Super Chef," according to Juliette Rossant, author of a book of the same name. "More capital was available for risky ventures like restaurants," wrote Rossant, and chefs learned "media-savvy ways." Like Lagasse and Prudhomme and their seasonings, they created their own lines of products. Rick and Deann Bayless's Frontera Foods manufactured salsas and, later, pizzas. Trotter packaged his citrus-cured salmon, sauces, and salad dressings for gourmet shops and supermarkets, as well as his own takeout shop, Trotter's To Go. Having a chef's name on a product was the "food world's equivalent of a designer logo," according to supermarket guru Phil Lempert.

Chefs also took up the notion of "vertical" food presentation that had become so popular in New York City and elsewhere. Stacks of layered meats, vegetables or pastry challenged diners to eat them without destroying them. Garnishes were elaborate, and dinner plates became canvases for brilliantly colored sauces.

While some of the city's chefs went vertical, others went horizontal—in the form of plate-filling steaks. Although many diners gave lip service to healthy eat-ing, they still were chowing down on huge slabs of red meat. Gene & Georgetti's, Morton's, Gibson's, and the Chicago Chop House are home-grown steak-houses that draw huge crowds. The steak appeal con-tinued throughout the decade and into the next.

SPICY CHINESE RIBS

Chicago's Chinatown has always fascinated me. After a stroll down crowded Wentworth Street, I usually opt for a restaurant that offers fiery treats like these spicy ribs. Chinese restaurant chefs usually twice-fry pork spareribs in hot oil to create a brown and crispy exterior. At home, I prefer to roast tender back ribs at a high temperature. Lots of the fat rendered from the ribs will be left behind on the baking sheet, which is an added bonus. Serve these flavorful morsels as part of an Asian buffet dinner or as zesty appetizers at casual parties—and pass plenty of napkins.

—JeanMarie Brownson

- 2 slabs (about 3½ pounds) baby back pork ribs
  Salt and freshly ground black pepper, to taste
- 3 tablespoons Chinese black bean garlic sauce (such as Lee Kum Kee brand)
- 3 tablespoons Chinese rice wine (Shaoxing) or pale, dry sherry
- 2 to 3 teaspoons crushed red pepper flakes (depending on your penchant for spice)
- 2 teaspoons sugar
- 2 to 3 tablespoons peanut oil
- 2 tablespoons sesame seeds
- 1 tablespoon toasted sesame oil
- 1 teaspoon hot chili oil, optional
  Green onions and cilantro leaves, chopped, for garnish

Preheat the oven to 375°F on a convection setting or 400°F on a regular setting. Cut the ribs into single-rib pieces. Arrange in a single, uncrowded layer on two jelly roll pans. Sprinkle all sides of the ribs with salt and pepper. Roast until nicely browned and crisp, about 40 minutes.

Meanwhile, mix the bean sauce, rice wine, pepper flakes, and sugar in a small dish. Heat a large well-seasoned wok or skillet until hot. Add the peanut oil; heat until hot. Add the ribs and stirfry 1 or 2 minutes. Add the chili-paste mixture and stirfry until fragrant, 1 or 2 minutes. Add the sesame seeds and stirfry another minute or so. Remove from heat; add the sesame oil and hot chili oil and mix well.

Arrange the ribs on a serving platter. Sprinkle with the onions and cilantro. Serve hot or at room temperature.

Makes 8 to 10 appetizer servings.

Note

To substitute spareribs, cut the ribs into single-rib pieces. Place in a large Dutch oven and add cold water to cover the ribs by 1 inch. Generously salt and pepper the water. Heat to a simmer over medium heat. Reduce the heat to low and cook, partly covered, 30 minutes or until almost tender. Skim off any foam that rises to the surface during cooking. Meanwhile, heat the oven to 400°F. Remove the ribs from the water and arrange on two jelly roll pans in a single, uncrowded layer. Roast, until nicely browned and tender, 30 to 40 minutes.

GENUINE APPLE STRUDEL

Old-world nostalgia keeps the German tradition alive today in Chicago. Not to be forgotten is our love of apfelstrudel. *The strudel served in most restaurants today and the recipes that use phyllo dough or frozen puff pastry are a far cry from the genuine strudel I watched my grandmother create. It helps to see it done once, but the technique is not difficult. Try it with a friend or two around to help. Enjoy your masterpiece warm "mit schlag" (with whipped cream).*

— Barbara Glunz

DOUGH:

2   cups all-purpose flour
1   large egg, at room temperature
⅔   cup warm water (105-115°F)
    Pinch salt
1   tablespoon butter, melted

FILLING:

1   cup sultana or golden raisins
½   cup ruby port wine

4   Granny Smith apples (about 2 pounds total), peeled, cored, thinly sliced
1   cup toasted fresh bread crumbs (see note)
    Grated rind (colored part only) of 1 lemon
¾   cup granulated sugar
1   teaspoon ground cinnamon
½   cup (1 stick) butter, melted and cooled
1   cup slivered almonds
    Confectioners' sugar for sprinkling on top

For the dough, place the flour in the bowl of a food processor. Beat the egg with the water, salt, and the 1 tablespoon melted butter. With the machine running, pour the egg mixture into the food processor, then process for 30 seconds. Turn the dough out onto a floured surface and knead it just enough to coat it with flour. Shape the dough into a ball. Place in a large bowl; cover and let rest 30 to 60 minutes.

For the filling, soak the raisins in the port in a small bowl. Combine the apples with the bread crumbs and lemon rind in a large bowl. Combine the granulated sugar and cinnamon in a small bowl. Have the other ingredients measured and drain the raisins before beginning to stretch the dough. Butter a large baking pan.

Preheat the oven to 400°F. Cover a 36-inch square table with a clean cloth; dust the cloth with flour. Roll out the dough to a 12-inch circle. Brush the surface with 1 tablespoon melted butter. Then, begin stretching dough with the backs of your hands by first centering them under the dough with fists closed, knuckle to knuckle. Raise the dough to chest level with elbows bent and slowly pull your fists 6 inches apart, extending your fingers to support the dough as it stretches. Return the dough to the table, rotate it 90°, and repeat the action until the dough is thin in the center and measures 24 inches in diameter.

Continue stretching the dough, moving your closed fists from the center toward yourself as the dough rests on the table. Circle the table as you work so the dough stretches evenly. Pinch closed any small tears in the dough; larger tears may be patched later with excess dough from the edges.

When the dough reaches the edge of the table, place your hands under the dough and let your fingers and the weight of the dough gently pull it down the sides. When the dough has stretched 8 to 10 inches down the sides, stop and trim off the thick excess edges to within 2 inches of the tabletop, saving pieces to patch holes.

Brush the stretched dough with the 2 tablespoons of melted butter. Lay the apples in a strip along one side of the stretched dough, covering a quarter of the dough. Cover the apples with drained raisins and slivered almonds. Sprinkle ⅔ of the cinnamon-sugar mixture over the apples.

Holding the cloth firmly with both hands along the filled edge, lift the cloth and gently fold up the strudel. After two folds, turn up the edges at both ends to close them and continue folding. Form the strudel into a horseshoe shape and slide it onto a buttered baking pan. Brush with the remaining melted butter. Sprinkle with the remaining cinnamon-sugar mixture and make decorative cuts in several places to release steam.

Bake until golden brown, 45 to 50 minutes. Cool on a wire rack. Sprinkle with confectioners' sugar. Serve warm, but never reheat in the microwave, as this will toughen the pastry.

Makes about 16 servings.

Note

To toast bread crumbs, spread them on a baking sheet and bake in a 325°F oven for 10 minutes.

SWEDISH LACE OATMEAL COOKIES

I know in today's culinary world, it seems almost ordinary to enjoy foods from other countries. But it wasn't always that way. When I was a food editor at the Chicago Sun-Times *from 1957 to 1965, I remember the gradual introduction of recipes for ethnic foods into my section. Today, many people enjoying cooking all kinds of foods. Havrekakor, a luscious cookie from Sweden, is one of the simplest and best cookies I know.*

—Alma Lach

¼ cup (½ stick) unsalted butter, at room temperature
  Dash salt
½ cup granulated sugar
1½ cups quick cooking oatmeal

Preheat the oven to 375°F. Combine all the ingredients in a large mixing bowl; stir well.

Line baking sheets with parchment paper or silicone baking mats. Drop the batter by teaspoonfuls onto each baking sheet about 2 inches apart. Bake until lightly browned around the edges, about 5 minutes. Remove the pan from the oven and let cookies cool for 1 minute before gently lifting them to a rack to cool.

Makes about 6 to 7 dozen cookies.

Note

The oatmeal flakes should be whole. Do not use the powdery oats in the bottom of the box, because they thicken the dough; the cookies will not spread and become lacy. If necessary, sift the oatmeal to use only the whole flakes.

THE MELTING POT

But steak and fine dining still remained an occasional treat for most diners in the '90s. Where else were they eating? In ethnic storefront cafés, just as Chicagoans had been doing for decades. The city's neighborhoods always have drawn diners in search of hearty fare at bargain prices. As immigrants move to the region, they bring their food traditions with them, and many open shops and restaurants that serve their specialties—anything from Italian sausages to Greek moussaka to Vietnamese pho. All the diverse cultures and traditions of the world flavor Chicago's melting pot.

"It was no casual decision that brought my grandfather to North Wells Street in the 1880s," relates current Les Dames Chicago president Barbara Glunz-Donovan, who is now the owner of the wine and liquor shop he opened there. "This was *the* German neighborhood. Oscar Mayer and Dr. Scholl, just to the north, employed hundreds of German-speaking immigrants. On Lincoln Avenue, Chicagoans found a string of ethnic bakeries and beer gardens, and a vibrant German press. In 1900, one out of every four Chicago residents, or one or both of their parents, had been born in Germany." Glunz-Donovan remembers going to The Red Star Inn, which offered delicious sauerbraten and melt-in-your-mouth apple pancakes and survived into the 1960s, and the Germania Club, which now has landmark status.

From the early 1980s on, The Golden Ox on North Halsted Street had been a reliable destination for traditional German fare, competing with its downtown rival, the venerable Berghoff Restaurant. Other popular ethnic restaurants of the day included The Bagel in Albany Park; Ann Sather on Belmont and the Swedish restaurants of Andersonville; Greek Islands in Greektown; Nuevo Leon in Pilsen; Gladys's Luncheonette and Army & Lou's for soul food on the South Side; and Uno's or Gino's East pizzerias located near the Magnificent Mile. Other tiny cafes dished up Italian, Thai, Polish, East Indian, Lebanese, Chinese, Japanese, Korean, Filipino cuisine and more.

"If New York is the Big Apple, then Chicago could aptly be called the Big Potato, or better yet, the Big Piroshki," according to *Where to Eat in America*. "To find a complete soup-to-strudel spread for under $3, just take a trip down Milwaukee Avenue for a Polish version, Chicago Avenue for Ukrainian, Marquette Park or Bridgeport for Lithuanian, or follow Cermak Road out to the Bohemian dumpling domain of Berwyn. The melting pot refuses to stop bubbling."

ETHNIC RESTAURANTS DOMINATE

In the '80s, ethnic food began to escape the neighborhoods. Ethnic ingredients were finding their way into mainstream supermarkets, and they also became sought after by more Chicago diners. BYOB places that featured little-known foods such as Hungarian *gulyas* or Ethiopian *injera* suddenly became popular. As people traveled more and tasted exotic foods, they became willing to sample these new dining opportunities at home.

Vietnamese and Thai restaurants began appearing everywhere—both downtown and out in the neighborhoods. Pad Thai soon became one of Chicago's favorite dishes. The fine-dining Thai restaurant

CREOLE RED BEANS AND RICE

Recipes from Mobile, Alabama, where my family lived for five generations, tend to offer their own unique blend of Caribbean, French, Spanish, Native American, Italian, and African influence. My grandmother used black beans as often as red beans in her bean-and-rice dishes. Mobile's hot sausages more closely resembled smoked Spanish-style chorizo or Portuguese chorico than the andouille sausages that are popular in New Orleans Creole cooking. You'll find red beans and rice in many of Chicago's soul food restaurants. —Donna Pierce

1	pound dried red beans, kidney beans, or black beans	1	teaspoon ground cumin
3	tablespoons olive oil, divided	½	teaspoon ground allspice
1	rib celery, finely chopped	¼	teaspoon freshly ground black pepper
1	large onion, finely chopped	1	pound smoked Creole hot sausages (andouille) or Spanish-style chorizo (not Mexican), sliced ¼-inch thick
3	cloves garlic, minced		
1	can (14½ ounces) chicken broth	¼	cup chopped fresh cilantro
1	can (14½ ounces) diced tomatoes, drained	1	tablespoon fresh thyme leaves
1	bay leaf	1	teaspoon salt
		3	cups hot cooked rice

Cover the beans with water in a large bowl; cover loosely with a cloth. Let soak for about 12 hours. Drain the beans.

Heat 2 tablespoons of the oil in a Dutch oven over medium heat. Add the celery and onion; cook, stirring, until the celery and onions soften, about 6 minutes. Add the garlic; cook, stirring, 1 minute. Add the chicken broth and tomatoes; stir in the beans. Add enough cold water just to cover (about 4 cups). Add the bay leaf, cumin, allspice, and black pepper. Heat to a boil; reduce heat to a simmer. Cover; cook until the flavors come together, about 20 minutes.

Meanwhile, heat the remaining 1 tablespoon of oil in a large skillet over medium-high heat; add the sausage. Reduce heat to medium. Cook, stirring occasionally, until the sausages begin to brown around the edges, about 8 minutes. Transfer to a plate lined with paper towels. Discard all except 1 tablespoon of oil. Stir the cilantro and thyme into the oil over medium-high heat. Cook, stirring, about 1 minute. Turn off the heat; set the mixture aside.

Stir the reserved sausage slices into the beans. Recover the pot. Cook until the beans are tender, about 1¼ hours. Remove the bay leaf; stir in the reserved cilantro-thyme mixture and salt. Serve over rice.

Makes 8 servings.

Arun's, which opened in 1985, became so popular that owner Arun Sampanthavivat moved to a larger space on Kedzie Avenue on the Northwest Side in 1988. His artful plates of Thai food matched the simple, beautiful Thai artwork and décor in the new spot. He soon gained attention from local and national restaurant critics, while smaller mom-and-pop restaurants began to dot the North Side.

Mexican food continued to be popular, and like the Baylesses, a few restaurateurs moved beyond the usual Tex-Mex style to more adventuresome regional dishes. Maria Josefa Concannon's Northwest Side

A TASTE OF POLAND

Chicago's Polish population is second only to that of Warsaw. There was a large emigration of Poles, Lithuanians, Romanians, and Ukrainians from the late 1880s to about 1914, and these closely-knit people brought their culinary traditions to the New World. The Poles settled along Milwaukee Avenue, and even today many Polish shops, restaurants, and businesses line that diagonal street. A large Polish community is centered near Belmont and Central, and another Polish enclave remains along Archer Avenue on the South Side.

In the 1970s, I was asked by Dale Brown, who was writing a chapter on Chicago's Polish neighborhoods for the Time-Life Foods of the World series, to act as a tour guide. As food editor of the Chicago Sun-Times, I had written about Polish cuisine before and was glad to assist. He wrote about our day of touring in his book, American Cooking: The Melting Pot.

We visited a Polish bakery and a Polish sausage shop on Division Street, near Ashland and Milwaukee Avenues, and had lunch at Turewicz. The restaurant tasting included clear, lemon-flavored beet borscht, which is traditionally served with *uszka*, tiny ear-shaped meat-filled dumplings; *golabki* (literally, little pigeons), stuffed cabbage rolls in a mushroom sauce; *zraziki*, which is beef pounded thin and rolled around bread stuffing with a slice of pickle; and *kasza*, buckwheat groats. We also enjoyed *bigos* (hunter's stew), which is traditionally prepared from game, but our version contained pork, bacon, and slices of kielbasa cooked with sauerkraut and was seasoned with onions and garlic. We ate delicious *nalesniki* (thin, filled pancakes) filled with farmer's cheese and strawberry or cherry jam and then rolled. We finished with *krupnik*, a spiced honey liqueur. —*Camille Stagg*

Mexican spot, Don Juan's, thrived under the kitchen skills of her son, chef Patrick Concannon.

Concannon's restaurant, she said, was born out of a sense of frustration. She was a Montessori teacher, but after a divorce she was having a hard time making ends meet and needed to make extra money.

"I come from a Mexican family of intellectuals, but had to work in all kind of jobs in restaurants— from waitressing to catering—and for my last job, I hostessed at a Mexican restaurant. The food there was so bad that I said to myself, 'I can do it better!' She found a small vacant restaurant space and opened her first place, but soon found she needed more space. "I

then found a bigger place, but needed money for it and I called my father," she said. "He thought at first that I needed the money for going back to school, but once he found out what it was for, I just heard silence. He was shocked. But he gave in. I so wish that he could see what Patrick and I accomplished. Without the support of my family, Don Juan would not be possible."

Another fine Mexican spot, Salpicon, opened on Wells Street; there, Priscila Satkoff produced upscale regional Mexican dishes. Hinsdale boasted Salbute, which offered a modern Mexican menu in a bistro-like setting. Chef Geno Bahena, who had worked for the Baylesses at Frontera Grill and Topolobampo, drew customers to his own restaurants, Chilpancingo and Ixcapuzalco.

Emilio Gervilla opened a tapas place in Hillside named Emilio's, which marked the beginning of his popular chain of Spanish restaurants in the city and suburbs. Pan-Latin American fare began to catch on with places such as Nacional 27 and Mas.

Trumping them all, however, was the call of rustic ragu, risotto, and the ubiquitous penne with vodka sauce. Italian cooking in the many trattorias and ristorantes around the city captivated Chicagoans, and northern Italian cuisine reigned. When Spiaggia opened, some marveled at the steep prices charged for simple Italian dishes. (They may have been simple, but they were exquisitely so.) At Avanzare, chef Dennis Terczak introduced Chicagoans to such exotics as carpaccio, tenette with smoked goose, and grilled radicchio with pine nuts. It was no spaghetti-and-meatballs place.

Chinese food experienced a similar boom. Sticking with a straightforward upscale Chinese theme, Lettuce Entertain You opened Ben Pao in 1996; the restaurant featured a tea bar, a sleek dining room, and ritzy Chinese dumplings, ribs, and stir-fries with prices way above any in Chinatown. Jerry Kleiner opened Opera, a huge, dramatic space with hip Chinese fare in the booming South Loop area.

Chicago's love of sushi seemed to transcend all the other Asian foods, however. By the mid-'90s, it became apparent that raw fish was here to stay. The Old Town staple Kamehachi had always been a hard table to get, but now countless other sushi spots popped up in profusion to ease the rush. And as they multiplied, they also went upscale. "The Japanese

juggernaut rolls on," Chicago's *Zagat Guide* announced in 2005. Joining restaurants such as Heat, Sushi Wabi and Kuni's were Kaze Sushi, Tsuki, Kuzoku, Meiji, and many more. Almost 50 sushi restaurants were listed in the 2005 *Zagat.*

Meanwhile, casual French bistros came back, continuing the tradition begun earlier by George Badonsky's Bastille, Bob Djahanguiri's Yvette, and Sue Gin's Café Bernard. A string of casual French restaurants where steak frites and tarte tatin often graced paper-topped tables popped up: Kiki's Bistro, Le Bouchon, Cyrano's Bistrot, Café 36, Bistro 110, and many more. Monique Hooker opened Monique's Café, with an all-French menu in a loft building north of Chicago Avenue; she often held French cooking classes at the restaurant as well.

There were so many cuisines to pick from in the city. Joan Reardon and Deborah Reeves wrote in *Crossroads '97*, a guide to Chicago, that "there is an eclectic ethnic vitality in Chicago, perhaps more than any other American city, which translates into a culinary heaven for the adventurous."

MORE CASUAL FARE

By the end of the 1990s and into the next decade, fast-food and casual restaurants were changing their menus, according to Beverly Bundy, author of *The Century in Food: America's Fads and Favorites.* Americans were spending 50 percent of their dining-out dollar for fast food by the end of the '90s, and they were ready for more choices.

Some of the fine-dining trends were trickling down. They "began offering once-exotic items like Caesar salad. Southwestern fare refused to fade, and dishes such as tortilla soup were served by main-stream restaurants," Bundy wrote.

Fast-food restaurants and convenience markets also competed with each other by upping portion size, which signaled the beginning of the "super-size-it" trend—7-Eleven's foot-long hot dog, Burger King's Quad Stacker, and Hardee's Monster Thickburger (1,400 calories!).

New beverage options arrived in the form of juice bars, coffee shops, and a plethora of bottled waters, from fancy to flavored. At bars and nightclubs, cocktail culture—led by a martini renaissance—came

back to captivate a new generation with new and traditional drinks.

Breakfast and brunch became more popular than ever for dining out. The venerable Lou Mitchell's, located near Union Station, still offered free Milk Duds along with its great skillet omelets, but other popular restaurants offering an array of morning fare picked up steam, including Ina Pinkney's Ina's Restaurant, which had moved to the Randolph Street Market area, and the nearby Wishbone restaurant, with its Southern-style grits and gravy.

While Chicagoans will never give up their deep-

POLISH-STYLE FILLED PANCAKES

My mother, Jeanette Stagg, was born in Poznan, Poland, and arrived in the U.S. with her family at the tender age of 1. Her family settled in a Polish neighborhood on Chicago's Near North Side, where she grew up amidst the rich cultural traditions of her homeland, including nalesniki. *These pancakes are made with various fillings for parties: the beef version uses leftover roast for a family supper; the slightly sweet cheese variation works as a side dish or dessert. The sweet pancakes are especially loved by Mom's grandchildren.*   —Camille Stagg

PANCAKES:

½	cup milk	Dash salt
½	cup water	Oil
1	egg, lightly beaten	Beef Filling or Sweet Cheese Filling (recipes follow)
1	egg yolk, lightly beaten	1 tablespoon butter, divided
¾ to 1 cup all-purpose flour		Sour cream or plain yogurt, for serving

For the pancakes, whisk together the milk, water, egg, and egg yolk in a medium bowl. Stir in the flour and salt until blended. Cover; let rest about 20 minutes. The batter should be thin; add more water if necessary.

Lightly oil a 7-inch crepe pan or nonstick skillet; heat until hot. Pour in 3 to 4 tablespoons of the batter, rotating the skillet quickly so the batter covers the bottom of the pan completely and evenly. Cook over medium heat until golden-brown on bottom, about 30 seconds. Using a wide spatula, turn quickly and cook the second side until golden brown, about 20 seconds more. Remove to a hot platter, cover, and keep warm while repeating the process until all the batter is used.

Divide Beef or Sweet Cheese Filling among pancakes and roll up. Melt half the butter in the same skillet.

dish pizza, the thin crust version started gaining ground with the 2006 arrival of a few pizzerias with wood-burning ovens in classic Neapolitan style. Spacca Napoli, in the Ravenswood area, and Crust, an all-organic pizzeria from chef Michael Altenberg, are just two places that are focused on Italian-style pizzas.

For comfort food, diners flocked to Bucktown's Hot Chocolate from Mindy Segal, and, for hot dogs with a twist, to Hot Doug's. For quite some time, it seemed that one or two great restaurants opened every week in the city or suburbs.

LIGHTENING UP

"Small plates" began to appear in more upscale restaurants, taking a cue from the popular Spanish tapas concept. People liked the idea of sharing plates and sampling dishes. Wine-focused restaurants offered half-glasses of wine and wine flights, so patrons could sample a wider variety.

The food also reflected the growing sophistication of the customers. In her book *The Eclectic Gourmet Guide to Chicago*, Camille Stagg noted, "food in restaurants is lighter, with flavoring coming from fresh herbs, spices, infused oils, vinaigrettes and

---

Add 3 or 4 rolled pancakes, brown quickly; repeat the procedure with the remaining butter and pancakes. Serve with the sour cream.

Makes 6 to 8 servings.

BEEF FILLING

- 1 tablespoon butter
- 2 to 2¼ cups (about 1 pound) cooked ground beef or leftover roast beef, chopped
- 1 medium onion, chopped
- 1 tablespoon chopped fresh dill
- 1 tablespoon chopped fresh parsley
  Salt and freshly ground black pepper, to taste
- 2 to 4 tablespoons beef broth

Heat the butter in a medium skillet. Add the beef and onion; cook until browned. Stir in the dill, parsley, salt, and pepper. Add the 2 tablespoons broth and stir; continue adding as much broth as the meat will absorb. Cover and simmer over low heat for a few minutes. Use to fill the pancakes.

Makes about 2½ cups.

SWEET CHEESE FILLING

- 1¾ cups dry cottage cheese
- 3 egg yolks
- 1 tablespoon butter, melted
- ¼ cup granulated sugar
- 1 teaspoon grated orange rind (colored part only)
- 1 teaspoon pure vanilla extract
- ¼ cup golden raisins, optional

Combine the cottage cheese, yolks, and butter in a medium bowl until blended. Stir in the sugar, orange rind, vanilla, and raisins; mix well. Use to fill the pancakes.

Makes 2 cups.

CHICAGO-STYLE STUFFED SPINACH PIZZA

This stuffed pizza is a version of the iconic deep-dish pizza so familiar to Chicagoans; it has a bottom and top crust. Adapted from The Chicago Tribune Good Eating Cookbook.

CRUST:

2	envelopes (¼ ounce each) active dry yeast
1	tablespoon sugar
2	cups warm water (105-115°F)
⅓	cup vegetable oil
4 to 6	cups all-purpose flour
⅛	teaspoon salt

SAUCE:

2	tablespoons olive oil
1	clove garlic, minced
1	can (28 ounces) crushed tomatoes with purée
2	teaspoons dried oregano
1½	teaspoons dried basil
¼	teaspoon salt
¼	teaspoon freshly ground pepper

FILLING:

2½	cups shredded mozzarella cheese
3	packages (10 ounces each) frozen chopped spinach, thawed, drained well
8	ounces fresh mushrooms, sliced (optional)
½	cup freshly grated Parmesan cheese
½	cup freshly grated Romano cheese
2	garlic cloves, minced
2	tablespoons olive oil
1	teaspoon dried basil
¼	teaspoon salt
¼	teaspoon freshly ground pepper

For the crust, dissolve the yeast and sugar in water in a large bowl; set aside to stand until bubbly, about 5 minutes. Stir in the oil. Stir in 4 cups of the flour and the salt until smooth; stir in the remaining flour as needed until a stiff dough forms. Knead on a lightly floured surface until the dough is smooth and elastic, about 10 minutes. Put into a greased bowl; turn to coat the top. Let rise, covered, in a warm place until doubled in volume, about 1 hour.

For the sauce, heat the oil in a large saucepan over medium heat; add the garlic and cook 2 minutes. Stir in the tomatoes, oregano, basil, salt, and pepper. Simmer, stirring often, until very thick, about 30 minutes.

For the filling, set aside ½ cup of the mozzarella. Squeeze as much water out of the spinach as you can. Mix the spinach with the remaining filling ingredients in a large bowl.

Preheat the oven to 450°F. Punch down the dough. Let it rest 10 minutes. Roll ⅔ of the dough into a 16-inch circle. Fit into a lightly oiled 14-inch pizza pan (at least 2 inches deep); let the dough overhang the edges of the pan.

Sprinkle the reserved ½ cup mozzarella cheese over the bottom crust. Spoon the spinach filling into the center of the crust, then smooth it evenly to cover the surface. Roll the remaining dough into a 14-inch circle. Place in over the filling. Crimp the edges of the top and bottom crusts together; trim off any excess dough. Pour the sauce over the top crust. Bake until the sides of the pizza are nicely golden and the top crust is firm, 30 to 40 minutes. Let stand 10 minutes before cutting into wedges.

Makes 6 to 8 servings.

wines, and from healthful cooking methods such as grilling and roasting in wood-burning ovens."

Places with that lighter touch included Spruce, which featured former White House chef Keith Luce. Luce wowed the critics with eclectic dishes such as roulade of smoked rabbit and rabbit mousse wrapped in prosciutto. But after Luce left for Colorado, owner Dan Sachs eventually closed Spruce and moved on to open the popular Bin 36 wine bar and restaurant in the Marina City towers.

CHEF STARS

Rick Tramonto and Gale Gand, the founding chefs at Henry Adaniya's Evanston-based Trio, opened the sleek Tru in 1999 with Rich Melman as their partner; there, they served American-French food on eclectic

---

CHICAGO CHEDDAR DAWGS

In the city that loves hot dogs, the Chicago dog reigns supreme. A Vienna Beef frank is served on a poppy seed roll and "dragged through the garden," as true dog connoisseurs say. For the uninformed, that means your dog will be topped with yellow mustard, sweet pickle relish, chopped onion, fresh tomato, a pickle spear, peppers, and a dash of celery salt. The Chicago Cheddar Dawg featured here is a variation on that theme that appeals to cheeseheads everywhere!

—Elizabeth Karmel

Recipe adapted from *Taming the Flame: Secrets for Hot-and-Quick Grilling and Low-and-Slow BBQ* (John Wiley & Sons).

4 to 8 all-beef franks, preferably Vienna Beef	Chopped white onion
Cheddar cheese spread (such as Merkt's brand)	Fresh tomato slices
	Dill pickle spears
4 to 8 poppy seed hot dog rolls	Pickled peppers (pepperoncino)
Yellow mustard	Dash of celery salt
Sweet (neon green) pickle relish	

Build a charcoal fire or preheat a gas grill to medium-low heat. Place the hot dogs directly on the cooking grate and grill for 6 to 8 minutes, turning occasionally until brown and warmed through:

Remove from the grill and to the buns, while still very hot, spread them with a generous amount of the Cheddar cheese spread. Serve, Chicago-style, if desired, with a choice of any of the other ingredients as condiments.

Makes 4 to 8 servings.

Tip

Have you ever had hot dogs or sausages explode when you were grilling them/ If so, you are not alone. In fact, this common occurrence is exactly why the Brits call sausages bangers. The problem is easy enough to fix—make a few pinpoint holes with a toothpick in cold hot dogs and cook them over a medium-low heat. The holes let the steam escape, and the medium-low heat allows the dogs to slowly caramelize on the outside

CHOCOLATE PHYLLO STACK WITH
WHITE CHOCOLATE GANACHE AND RASPBERRIES

Julia Child telephoned me one day at work (you never needed to ask, "Who is it?" when she called), to ask if I would help her with a new book she was writing about pastry. She wanted me to be her "Phyllo Maven." I created a bunch of recipes using phyllo in many different ways, both savory and sweet. This is a version of a dessert I wrote for that book. Julia and I made it at her house in Cambridge as we filmed an episode of her TV show, "Baking with Julia." What an experience that was! — Gale Gand

6 ounces white chocolate, chopped	4 sheets phyllo (filo) dough, thawed according to package directions
1½ cups heavy (whipping) cream	
¼ cup unsweetened cocoa powder	½ cup granulated sugar for sprinkling
½ cup clarified butter (see note)	1 half pint raspberries
	Confectioners' sugar

Prepare the white chocolate ganache filling at least one day before you plan to serve the dessert.

Place the white chocolate in a medium bowl. Heat the cream in a small saucepan over medium heat just to a boil. Immediately turn off the heat. Pour the hot cream over the chocolate; whisk until the chocolate is melted and smooth. Strain into a small mixer bowl; cover and refrigerate overnight.

Preheat the oven to 350°F. Whisk together the cocoa powder and butter in a small bowl; keep warm. Line a 12- x 17-inch baking sheet with parchment paper. Place 1 sheet of phyllo on the pan and brush with the cocoa mixture. Sprinkle evenly with the 2 tablespoons of granulated sugar, then place another sheet of phyllo on top; continue layering to create 4 layers. Cover the stack with parchment paper. Place another baking sheet on top of the parchment paper (one slightly smaller than the bottom one) to weigh it down and to keep the phyllo from buckling during baking.

Bake until the phyllo is crispy, 12 to 15 minutes. Let cool on a wire rack, but do not unstack pans.

To serve, remove the white-chocolate mixture from the refrigerator. Beat the white-chocolate mixture with an electric mixer into fluffy, soft peaks; do not overwhip, or it will break down. Return to the refrigerator. Break off pieces of the phyllo stack into freeform pieces, each about 3 inches square. Place dabs of the ganache in the middle of 4 or 6 dessert plates. Place a piece of the phyllo stack onto the dab of ganache, then top the phyllo with another spoonful of ganache. Sprinkle with a few raspberries. Repeat the layering one more time, and top with a third piece of phyllo. Add more raspberries and sprinkle lightly with confectioners' sugar to serve.

Makes 4 to 6 servings.

Note

To clarify butter, bring it to a slow boil over low heat. Boil gently until the solids separate from the fat, about 10 minutes. Remove from heat; skim off the foam. Slowly pour off the clarified butter (the clear yellow liquid), leaving behind the residue of milk solids. Discard the milk solids.

tableware—including a caviar "tower"—and Gand's imaginative mini-desserts.

Tramonto and Gand were just two chefs of many that were adding to Chicago's growing reputation for fine food. There also was Carrie Nahabedian, who returned from Los Angeles to open her own restaurant, NAHA, in the old Gordon location in River North. Her seasonal American food with Mediterranean accents and French techniques was the perfect expression of her Armenian background, French training, and American experiences in some of the best restaurants in Chicago and around the country.

Shawn McClain attracted praise while working at Trio before leaving to start a string of restaurants: Spring, Green Zebra, and Custom House. Green Zebra was the city's first upscale vegetarian restaurant, and it made many true believers out of former carnivores.

The late 1990s and early 2000s brought in star out-of-town chefs such as David Burke with his Park Avenue Café, and later, Primehouse; Jean-Georges Vongerichten, with his Thai-influenced Vong (later renamed Vong's Thai Kitchen); and Douglas Rodriguez in 2006 with DeLaCosta.

Other home-grown stars who gained recognition during the period were Michael Taus at Zealous, Michael Kornick at MK, Bruce Sherman at North Pond, Paul Kahan at Blackbird, Mark Baker at Seasons, Suzy Crofton at Crofton on Wells, Susan Goss at West Town Tavern, Kevin Shikami of Kevin, and many more.

MAKING ROOM FOR FUSION

In 1982, two restaurants opened that foretold of a dining trend that would sweep Chicago during the next 20 years: fusion food. French cuisine-trained Yoshi Katsumura opened Yoshi's Café after working in many other Chicago restaurants, including Le Bastille, La Reserve, Le Francais, and Jimmy's Place. His Franco-Japanese fare offered pleasing contrasts of textures and unusual flavor combinations: breast of pheasant stuffed with pheasant mousse and served with a shiitake mushroom sauce, and green-tea ice cream long before it became a mainstream dessert. In Lincoln Park, Jackie Shen (then Jackie Etcheber) opened Jackie's, which specialized in nouvelle French seafood with Chinese influences, such as striped sea bass with shrimp, avocados, and peppers, or a phyllo nest with exotic mushrooms served with tomato basil-butter sauce. Her most famous dish became the chocolate "bag," which was filled with white chocolate mousse. She still serves the dish today as the chef at Red Light.

The fusion movement continued to build throughout the States in the 1990s as chefs were "deliberately blending cuisines," aided by an increasingly international food supply, as Lovegren noted in *Fashionable Food*. Japonais opened on the Chicago River in a sumptuously designed space in the old Montgomery Ward warehouse, and there, French cooking techniques mixed with Japanese sauces and ingredients. Jeanne McInerney Lubeck's Bamboo Blue, located in the southwest suburb of Homewood, serves casual dishes like burgers, quesadillas, and chowders flavored with Asian ingredients. The trendy Sushisamba Rio on Wells Street mixes the unlikely duo of Brazilian and Japanese cuisine on its menu. In 2005, Arun Sampanthavivat joined forces with

ROASTED CHICKEN MEDITERRANEAN

This dish combines the flavors of Greece, Italy, and the South of France. A beautiful and robust dish, it is easy to prepare and perfect for a dinner party. You may simplify it or embellish it in many ways. The addition of artichokes, oven-cured tomatoes, and grilled Swiss chard are some of my personal favorites. I love to roast the chicken on the bone; you may choose to use boneless breast instead. At NAHA, I've done a version using chickens from Earthshine Farms in Michigan. Young chickens are great for this dish because they are more fragrant. This recipe reminds me of relaxing on the Riviera. When I was growing up, my mother Helen and my Aunt Pauline (who is Greek) made this dish often for our families to enjoy!

—Carrie Nahabedian

4	large bone-in chicken breast halves (about 12 ounces each)
⅔	cup chopped Italian parsley, divided
2	teaspoons coarse (kosher) salt, divided
½	teaspoon cracked black pepper
1	teaspoon dried oregano
2	sprigs fresh thyme
1	bay leaf
6	tablespoons olive oil, divided
2	lemons
4	medium Idaho potatoes (about 8 ounces each)
2	cloves garlic, halved
½	cup white wine or dry vermouth
½	cup chicken stock or broth
¾	cup Kalamata olives, pitted
⅓	cup sun-dried tomatoes packed in oil, chopped, drained
¼	cup julienned fresh basil

Place the chicken in a deep dish or bowl. Add ⅓ cup of the chopped parsley, 1 teaspoon salt, cracked black pepper, dried oregano, thyme, bay leaf, and 4 tablespoons of the olive oil. Roll the lemons on the tabletop back and forth to loosen up the juices. Cut 1 lemon in half and squeeze the juice over the chicken; cut up the squeezed lemon halves and add to the chicken. Mix so the chicken pieces are nicely coated. Refrigerate 2 to 4 hours.

Preheat the oven to 350°F. Rinse the potatoes and pat dry. Cut each potato lengthwise into 8 wedges. Heat the remaining 2 tablespoons olive oil in a large, heavy, well-seasoned or nonstick skillet over medium heat. Add the potatoes in single uncrowded layer (work in batches if necessary). Cook, turning, until browned on all sides, about 10 minutes. Transfer the potatoes to a roasting pan large enough to hold the chicken and potatoes.

Remove the chicken from the marinade. Working in the same skillet, brown the chicken thoroughly on all sides, adding additional oil if necessary, about 10 to 15 minutes. Transfer the chicken to the roasting pan with the potatoes. Add the garlic and season everything with remaining 1 teaspoon salt. Pour any drippings from the skillet over the chicken and potatoes. Roast the chicken and potatoes until the chicken is tender and tests done (165°F internal temperature), 20 to 30 minutes.

Transfer the chicken and potatoes to a serving platter and keep warm. Set the roasting pan over medium-high heat and add white wine. Heat to a boil while scraping up browned bits from the bottom of the pan. Add the chicken stock, Kalamata olives, sun-dried tomatoes, basil, the remaining ⅓ cup Italian parsley, and the juice of the remaining lemon; heat through. Season to taste with salt and pepper. Spoon over the chicken and serve.

Makes 4 servings.

Roland Liccioni as consultants for the French-Vietnamese restaurant Le Lan (The Orchid) on Clark Street. Vermilion mixes Latin and South Asian dishes on one menu; ceviche and curries peacefully coexist on its menu.

THE 21ST CENTURY ARRIVES

At the turn of the century, chefs were taking "pride in seeking out small, quality purveyors and changing their menus to utilize the freshest of seasonal ingredients and more organic ingredients," wrote Stagg in

---

MIXED VEGETABLE CURRY

This curry is an excellent way to get your vegetables in the middle of a Chicago winter, when driving through the ice and snow to Devon Avenue's Indian restaurants proves treacherous. This is also a great accompaniment to grilled chicken. I like to make a rub of the same seasonings with a bit of sea salt and rub it into the chicken pieces before grilling.   —JeanMarie Brownson

1 teaspoon turmeric	2 large Yukon gold potatoes, cut into ½-inch cubes, unpeeled (12 ounces)
1 teaspoon ground coriander	2 cups skinny frozen green beans
1 teaspoon fenugreek seeds	1 small zucchini, halved, sliced ¼ inch thick
½ teaspoon cayenne pepper	1 small yellow squash, halved, sliced ¼ inch thick
½ teaspoon ground cumin	2 banana peppers, cut into ½-inch-wide strips
¼ teaspoon fennel seed	1 can (15 ounces) garbanzo beans, drained
¼ cup vegetable oil	About 1½ teaspoons salt
1 large sweet onion, halved, cut into thick wedges	1 teaspoon sugar
2 medium carrots, peeled, sliced ¼-inch thick	Chopped fresh cilantro for garnish
1 small (about 1 pound) butternut squash, peeled, seeded, cut into ½-inch cubes	Cooked basmati rice for serving
3 cloves garlic, minced or crushed	
1 can (14 ounces), or 1¾ cups, vegetable broth	

Grind the spices together in a small mortar to crush the seeds. Heat the oil in a large Dutch oven over medium-high heat. Add the onion and stir-fry until lightly golden, 5 or 6 minutes. Add the spices and stir-fry about 15 seconds; do not allow the spices to burn. Add the carrots, butternut squash, and garlic; stir well. Add the broth; heat to simmer. Simmer, partly covered, 10 minutes. Stir in the potatoes and green beans and simmer until all the vegetables are tender, about 10 minutes more.

Gently stir in the zucchini, yellow squash, banana peppers, garbanzos, and salt. (Add a little more broth if the mixture looks dry.) Cook and stir over medium-high heat until the zucchini is almost tender, about 5 minutes. Season with the sugar (and more salt if needed). Transfer to a serving dish. Garnish with the cilantro. Serve with the cooked basmati rice.

Makes 6 servings.

The Eclectic Gourmet Guide to Chicago. Esteemed Ritz-Carlton Dining Room chefs Sarah Stegner and George Bombaris left the hotel to open their own place, Prairie Grass Café in Northbrook, where they featured American dishes prepared with local, sustainably produced ingredients.

MOLECULAR GASTRONOMY

But there was another new movement afoot. Taking cues from the great Spanish chef Ferran Adria at El Bulli restaurant, chefs in Chicago began "playing" with their food. Using foams and sprays, and dissecting dishes in their kitchen labs, they presented extraordinary tasting menus—one item more bizarre than the next—to amaze diners. Some diners liked this new "molecular gastronomy," and some didn't. At the avant-garde Moto, chef Homaro Cantu created a menu that shocked many, especially when a dish of

VENISON MEDALLIONS WITH MUSHROOM HERB TOPPING

I brought this dish to one of our Les Dames holiday dinners; it's a home version of a classic venison dish.

—Sarah Stegner

4 medallions of venison loin or beef tenderloin filets (about 6 ounces each)	1 cup peeled minced shallots
Salt and black pepper, freshly ground, to taste	½ teaspoon minced garlic
1 tablespoon olive oil	¼ cup (½ stick) unsalted butter, at room temperature
TOPPING:	¼ cup fresh bread crumbs, toasted
2 cups fresh mushrooms, sliced	2 tablespoons chopped fresh Italian parsley
1 tablespoon olive oil	1 teaspoon chopped fresh chives
Salt and freshly ground black pepper, to taste	1 teaspoon chopped fresh tarragon

Preheat the oven to 400°F. Season the meat with salt and pepper. Heat a large skillet over medium-high until hot. Add the olive oil and heat, then add the medallions. Do not overcrowd. Cook the medallions, turning once, until the outside forms a crust, about 2 minutes per side. Transfer the medallions to a rack set over a baking sheet; set aside.

For the topping, add the mushrooms to the same skillet; season with salt and pepper. Cook over medium-high heat until the mushrooms are golden brown, about 5 minutes. Transfer to a cutting board and chop finely. Add the shallots to the same skillet. Cook until translucent and tender, about 5 minutes. Add the garlic and cook another minute. Remove the pan from heat. Combine the mushrooms and shallots in a medium bowl; mix well. When cool, add the butter, bread crumbs, and herbs; mix well. Taste and adjust the seasoning.

Divide the topping among the medallions. Roast until the medallions are medium-rare (about 145°F on an instant-read thermometer), 10 to 12 minutes. Serve on warm plates.

Makes 4 servings.

raw bass "baked tableside" arrived at the table. The Peninsula Hotel's Avenues restaurant got a shake-up when chef Graham Elliot Bowles and his equally experimental cuisine came on board.

Science in the city's restaurant kitchens reached a peak when, in 2004, Grant Achatz left Trio in Evanston to open his own place, Alinea, on Halsted Street in Chicago. Local critics loved the daring menu. In 2006, *Gourmet* magazine gushed: "Grant Achatz is redefining the American restaurant once again for an entirely new generation. And that— more than his gorgeous, inventive, and delicious food—is what makes Alinea the got-to-go-to restaurant in the country right now." The trend continues as more chefs rethink their dishes.

The big news among restaurateurs in 2006 was the controversial foie gras ban voted in by the city council. Charlie Trotter quietly stopped serving duck liver around 2002 on humanitarian grounds, as he believed that the force-feeding process that enlarges ducks' livers is inhumane. Chicago's aldermen took up the cause and proposed the ban. Other chefs in town insisted that they should be free to serve whatever foods they like; some disregarded the ban. The council's action followed the city's smoking ban in restaurants and preceded a proposal to ban the artery-clogging trans-fats used in so many quick-serve restaurants. Many critics charged that the city was legislating what Chicagoans could eat and it was simply going too far.

CHICAGO DINING EXPANDS

Meanwhile, many chefs and restaurateurs were expanding their businesses. Times seemed good. Several added Las Vegas properties, cashing in on the restaurant and bar boom there.

In 2006, Gale Gand and Rick Tramonto opened four new restaurants in a Wheeling hotel while still operating Tru in downtown Chicago. Tony Mantuano worked with Levy Restaurants on a 2007 opening in Miami of Enoteca Spiaggia. Charlie Trotter has plans to open two restaurants in the new Elysian Hotel on Walton Street in 2008 and continues to supervise his Restaurant C at the One and Only Palmilla Resort in Los Cabos, Mexico.

Paul Kahan of Blackbird and Avec planned a beer-focused restaurant for 2007 on Fulton Street. Along with Manny Valdes, JeanMarie Brownson, and Greg Keller, the Baylesses in 2006 opened Frontera Fresco in the State Street Macy's location with a small menu of Mexican street foods.

Chicago's dining scene simply keeps expanding, multiplying the opportunities for chefs and Chicagoans alike.

HOME COOKING

SOPHISTICATED FLAVORS

What were we cooking at home? At the beginning of the 1980s, it was mostly the basics, with some help from convenience products such as Hamburger Helper and cans of soup. As the decade advanced, Chicago's dinner tables reflected an increasing sophistication and a turn toward healthier fare.

On weekends, some cooked gourmet dinners for friends. Entertaining was easier, thanks to the food processor and other gourmet gadgets that began to appear in area cookware shops. Abby Mandel's "Machine Cuisine" food processor classes and her related cookbooks taught Chicagoans how to streamline their cooking with this revolutionary machine. Mandel traveled to Europe to cook with well-known chefs and returned home to translate and simplify their recipes for American cooks. Her books de-stressed many hostesses and helped make Cuisinart a household name.

At the same time, other cookbooks arrived to help harried cooks. *The Silver Palate Cookbook* by Julee Rosso and Sheila Lukins and Martha Stewart's *Entertaining* delivered easier, American-focused recipes for parties.

New ingredients helped cooks show off, too. Americans discovered importer Frieda Caplan's "new" fruit from New Zealand, the kiwi, and kiwi tarts popped up across the land. Other exotics began appearing in Chicago markets: passionfruit, mangoes, radicchio, enoki mushrooms, arugula, and green peppercorns. Ethnic staples and spices became increasingly easier to find in the city's supermarkets.

Through the 1980s and 1990s, Americans experimented with new flavors in their meals. Sales of salsa had already outstripped that of ketchup by $40 million by the early '90s. Chicago cooks soon learned the difference between habañeros and chipotles and poblanos and jalapeños. Mexican food remained a popular ethnic choice, along with Chinese, Thai, and Caribbean flavors. In many circles, Italian food gained popularity over French.

DINNER IN A FLASH

For the majority of time-pressed cooks, the grocery store's frozen-food case supplied dinner. In 1988, food companies introduced 972 new microwave-ready products, and microwave ovens were selling at a record pace, according to Lovegren. At the same time, fast-food giants like McDonald's, Kentucky Fried Chicken, and others drew more and more people out of their own kitchens.

The years of recession following the stock market crash of 1987 began the new decade on a gloomy note. Food prices rose. Money was tight, and although Americans did not entirely forsake their newfound habits of eating out more, most nights meant eating at home. Chicago newspapers often featured recipes for old-fashioned dishes they dubbed "retro-food." Inexpensive classics like casseroles, mashed potatoes, and meat loaf found their way back to the tables of many families.

By the mid-'90s, people were buying more take-out meals, and burritos and "wraps" made of tortillas or pita bread and fillings were challenging sandwiches as *the* lunchtime choice. Hand-held foods of all kinds became popular as people ate on the go, in the car, or at the office. "More and more, America wanted someone else to do the cooking," observed Bundy.

By the end of the 1990s, 70 percent of women were working outside the home. With less time in the kitchen, women modified their cooking and eating habits to fit their schedules and those of their family. The hectic lifestyle in the '90s led many experts to ask, "Will family dining survive?" The debate goes on today. No longer having time for "from scratch" cooking, women turned to "home-heated" meals from the market, or if they did cook, to convenience products. They got help from a slew of new cookbooks with titles such as "Desperation Dinners" and "Cooking 1-2-3: Fabulous Food Using Only 3 Ingredients." Others simply revved up the microwave for

an evening of Stouffer's or other frozen entrees in front of the TV.

More adventurous cooks turned to the hearty dishes of Italy: pastas, Tuscan beans, and risotto Milanese, for example. Trend-watcher Faith Popcorn and others called the trend of staying home and cooking "cocooning."

FOOD AND THE TUBE

With the creation of the Food Network in 1993, food—and chefs—became a media phenomenon. A cable channel solely devoted to food! Though the startup was slow and the programming had its critics, the channel was soon available in Chicago.

Cooks and noncooks alike became fascinated with Emeril Lagasse's bravado and, later, the competitive drama of *Iron Chef*. The Public Broadcasting System also added more cooking shows, including some with Charlie Trotter and Rick Bayless, as well as from Jacques Pepin, Martin Yan, Wolfgang Puck, and Martha Stewart, who "became the symbol of food and living for many," according to Bundy.

TRENDS IN HOME DINING AND ENTERTAINING

As the '90s progressed, the economy rebounded to new, technology-fueled heights, and people began to rise up from the couch and venture into their newly remodeled designer kitchens, often with glossy granite counters and high-end Viking ranges. It was an "age of excess," according to Jean Anderson, author of *The American Century Cookbook*. For many, cooking became entertainment once again, and lavish dinner parties made a comeback.

Grilling became the favorite way to entertain in the summer. More and more city balconies and suburban patios sported grills made by Palatine's Weber-Stephens Products Co., and the microwave oven (once the hope of so many cooks in the '70s and '80s) was increasingly relegated to heating leftovers.

People were traveling the world and bringing back new appreciation for the food of other countries. Cookbooks of all kinds sold well. In 1993, close to 1,000 new cookbooks were published, according to Traeger in *The Food Chronology*, and high sales continued throughout the 1990s. People simply were reading more about food than ever before, as they were often inspired by their own travels and the myriad cooking shows they watched on television. Food magazines such as *Cook's Illustrated*, *Fine Cooking* and *Saveur* joined *Gourmet* and *Bon Appetit* on the newsstands.

In 1997, the venerable *Joy of Cooking* got a major overhaul and expansion, and many Chicagoans contributed their expertise by writing segments of the new *Joy*, including Deann Bayless, JeanMarie Brownson, Jane Davis, Elaine González, Karen Levin, Nancy Ross Ryan, Jill Van Cleave, and Marilyn Wilkinson.

Newspapers began to take food more seriously, as consumer issues such as food safety, nutrition, and dieting became primary issues for millions of readers. "Food became a legitimate subject for journalists in the 1990s," said author Jean Anderson in a speech at a 2006 food writers' conference. In Chicago, editors such as Beverly Bennett and Carol Mighton Haddix followed the lead of previous food editors Alma Lach at the *Chicago Sun-Times* and Joanne Will at the *Chicago Tribune*. A new focus on consumerism—

especially health and nutrition advice—became standard in food sections of the time. "Certainly nutrition and the nutritional information on packaging became important," Lach said.

Wine was also getting plenty of press in the '90s. William Rice and his wife, Jill Van Cleave, a food consultant, moved from New York to Chicago when he joined the *Chicago Tribune* as a wine and food columnist after a stint as editor of *Food & Wine* magazine.

TRENDS IN CATERING

The booming economy at the end of the 20th century helped bring a return to luxury. Many people enjoyed eating out several nights a week with their newfound wealth, and Chicago-area caterers enjoyed the boom, as many people held lavish parties and events. Food continued to be a focus at charity events pulled together by caterers, event planners, and tabletop suppliers, many of them Les Dames members.

Jennifer Anderson started her own firm, Jennifer Anderson & Associates, which specializes in designing social and corporate special events. Her firm orchestrated a memorable evening of dinner and dancing in 2004 for Les Dames International at the Chicago Cultural Center. Linda J. Goodman's firm, Linda J. Goodman & Co, specializes in high-end weddings and corporate events around the country.

Wendy Pashman's The Entertaining Company is an award-winning catering firm in Chicago that does private parties and in-home events. And Kathy Ruff saw an opportunity—not for catering, but for supplying rentals for parties, such as complete tableware settings, glassware, chairs and tables with her firm, Tablescapes.

Rita Gutekanst opened Rita's Catering after working at Jerome's on Clark in Chicago. "I started catering really by accident," Gutekanst said. "While I was working at Jerome's, neighborhood folk began asking if we couldn't just bring some of the food from the restaurant and, oh yeah, some of the waiters, and serve the food at their party. After doing that a few times, I realized—wait a minute, this is catering. And so it began."

"All the changes in my own business have been because my clients have forced me to. As they traveled more, they wanted more and different ethnic foods served at their parties. I remember one client who asked for several French dishes that she had enjoyed on her recent travels. She was telling me the dishes she wanted in French and I was writing them down phonetically so I could go back to my chef and say 'do you know what this is, and can you do it?' Things are changing constantly in this business. Beef is the perfect example. There was a time when no one was serving beef at parties; just recently, we were serving it at every single party."

Gutekanst later changed her company's name to Limelight, and featured catered events with a natural food focus. "Our move toward more locally grown, natural, and seasonal foods was a logical next step. As I worked with the Green City Market and got to know the farmers, it was easy to understand how locally grown, fresh, seasonal food is better on many, many levels—taste included."

Unfortunately, the dot-com bust came calling just after Chicago celebrated a new millennium. For many, extra cash for fine dining and fancy foods dried up. As the new decade began, Americans once again found themselves cocooning with Boboli pizzas and macaroni and cheese (though now perhaps made with four cheeses instead of one).

HEALTH CONCERNS

As Chicagoans became more interested in what they ate, they became more interested in nutrition and its effect on their health. "By the 1980s, the young hippies who had espoused health food were aging baby boomers who had discovered that they could not only get old but could also fall prey to disease," noted Sylvia Lovegren in *The Oxford Encyclopedia of Food and Drink in America*. Oat bran, fiber, and monounsaturated fats were discovered to be good for health, and unsurprisingly, beef, butter, and eggs were not. Beef consumption dropped from 100 pounds per person in the 1970s to 70 pounds by the end of the 1980s, according to Lovegren.

Exercise and fitness took up more of the day's hours, and cooks turned to new magazines like *Cooking Light* for healthful dinner ideas. Some were ready to chuck the beef and used references like Oak Park's *Vegetarian Times* magazine. No longer considered an off-beat '60s phenomenon, vegetarianism began to make sense to more people.

In 1991, the USDA introduced the Food Pyramid, a simple teaching tool/graphic that replaced the old four basic food groups. The pyramid reflected the current thinking from scientists about what and how Americans should eat—fats and sugars at the "eat-less" top and grains at the "eat-more" base.

The pyramid was updated in 2005 to emphasize more physical activity, smaller portion size, and fewer calories. Grains, fruits, and vegetables were highlighted as desirable. The MyPyramid.gov website lets users key in their age, gender, and physical activity level to get personalized recommendations about their daily calorie level based on the 2005 Dietary Guidelines for Americans.

Mary Abbott Hess found herself at the forefront of educating consumers about food and nutrition. In the late 1970s, she started a consulting firm, Hess & Hunt Nutrition Communications, after serving as director of Mundelein College's food and nutrition program. She wrote nutrition books and cookbooks, including *Healthy Gourmet Cooking*; more recently, she helped develop recipes for Charlie Trotter's *Spa Cuisine*. She has also served as president of the American Dietetic Association.

"In the early '80s, people decided that fat was the big villain," Hess said. "And the food industry responded by creating food that people said they wanted—until they tasted it. Often manufacturers just replaced the fat with sugar, and ultimately most of these new low-fat and fat-free products were high-calorie failures. Throughout the decade, people just got fatter.

"Moving into the '90s, the type of fat in foods became a factor," she added. "The focus switched from saturated and polyunsaturated fats toward monounsaturated fats in 2000, and now it's all about trans fats. Popular diet plans in the '80s were very restrictive in fats—and people couldn't stick to them. In the '90s, they were very restrictive in carbs—and people couldn't stick to them, either. Now it seems that we are moving toward moderation. At least, I hope so!"

Nancy Kirby Harris, who started her career as a cooking teacher and caterer, also became involved in the health business, first in a position with the American Cancer Association and then as senior executive director at the American Diabetes Association, where she still oversees educational programming and fundraising. "People are learning more about nutrition—about what they can or cannot eat," she said. "It's all about balance, really." She also noted that the perception of diabetes has changed through the years. "It's taken much more seriously, and doctors now are diagnosing even pre-diabetes conditions in people."

In 1994, an obesity report by the National Center for Health Statistics of the Centers for Disease Control made headlines. According to the report, one in every three American adults was obese—an all-time high. The resulting concern about fat consumption prompted food firms to quickly bring new products to market, but not all of them were successful. Nabisco introduced a line of tremendously popular low-fat cookies called SnackWell's in 1993, but a few years later, demand dropped after nutritionists warned consumers about the high sugar content of many of the line's products. In 1996, Frito-Lay introduced a line of chips called WOW! that were made with a new oil called Olestra. Despite the line's initial popularity, interest dropped significantly as more consumers began to notice the following FDA-mandated warning on its packages:

"This product contains olestra. Olestra may cause abdominal cramping and loose stools. Olestra inhibits the absorption of some vitamins and other nutrients. Vitamins A, D, E, and K have been added."

By the end of the 1990s, vegetable consumption had dropped 16 percent from 1980s levels. This and other trends prompted the American Cancer Society's "Five a Day" campaign, which urged Americans to eat at least five servings of fruits and vegetables each day. As they became increasingly worried about getting enough fiber and nutrients, more people turned to their diets to take control of their health. Thus began the "functional foods" trend. "Nutraceutical" became a common term to describe foods with added vitamins, trace minerals, and plant extracts. Soon, food manufacturers were touting added doses of phytochemicals, such as lycopene from tomatoes or isoflavones from soybeans, to help protect consumers from cancer and other diseases.

Perhaps the most popular diet advice ever given in America came from doctors and authors who touted low-carbohydrate diets. The diet wasn't new, by any means, but it bounced back after Robert C. Atkins, author of 1972's *The Dr. Atkins Diet Revolution*, updated his plan for a new generation of dieters with the 2001 release *Dr. Atkins' New Diet Revolution*. Protein became the new buzzword as men and women stocked up on steaks, chops, and poultry. Chicago's steak houses rejoiced, and its bakeries were despondent. The phenomenon lasted well into the 2000s.

THE BUSINESS OF FOOD

STUDENTS OF FOOD

Chicagoans' interest in and desire to learn about food went through a series of ups and downs that were primarily tied to the vagaries of the economy. In the '50s and '60s, Antoinette Pope's School of Fancy Cookery had been the best-known school, and Pope had the first television cooking show in Chicago.

Alma Lach left the *Sun-Times* in 1964 to work on a cookbook; later, she worked as a consultant for Richard Melman's restaurants and for The Berghoff restaurant. In the 1970s, she also opened the Alma Lach Cooking School on Rush Street. " I remember Mayor [Michael] Bilandic and his wife waiting in their limo, creeping in at the last minute, sitting in the back row, and then leaving as soon as it was over," she said. "And then there was George Bay, who was in my school for a year; he went on to the Cordon Bleu for a year, and then back to work at Bay's English Muffins."

The Cook's Mart opened on a lonely stretch of LaSalle Street, but in time the shop attracted customers from all over the city and suburbs with its good selection of cookware and the classes taught in the store's modern demonstration kitchen. The owner was today's restaurant critic for the *Chicago Sun-Times*, Pat Bruno, who brought in nationally known teachers, such as Giuliano Bugialli and Diana Kennedy.

In the early 1980s, Elaine Sherman's shop, The Complete Cook, was ahead of its time. She opened the store in Glenview in 1976, and one year later, moved it to Deerfield; there, she sold hard-to-find pots, pans and utensils, as well as quality vinegars, oils, and other foodstuffs. The store quickly became *the* destination for the food community, remembered Nancy Kirby Harris, who taught classes there along with many other Les Dames members. "Elaine had read the market," Harris said. "She had tapped into the burgeoning interest in learning about great food—especially learning how to cook it." The Complete Cook offered cooking classes with many different instructors, including out-of-town food celebrities, such as Julia Child, Maida Heatter, and James Beard.

"My association with Elaine is a typical example of her sense of sharing and her belief in supporting those in the industry," said Harris. "One day I walked into The Complete Cook after recently returning from a stint at London's Cordon Bleu and was interested in pursing a career in the food business. Elaine showed me around the store and as the conversation turned to food, as most conversations with her did, we began discussing chili. Elaine expressed a desire to cook up a batch of great game chili. Little did she know that my husband at the time was a great game hunter, and I had hundreds of pounds of game in my freezer. I returned several days later with 25 pounds of elk and antelope—perfect ingredients for Elaine's chili. And so began our long association. Elaine became my mentor."

Madelaine Bullwinkel, a local cooking teacher, began her own cooking school, Chez Madelaine, in her home in 1977. "It began as a grass-roots endeavor," Bullwinkel recalled. "My classes were an extension of the baking and cooking techniques I felt secure about. I had no cooking degree at that time. My inspirations were Julia's *Mastering* volumes, her television series, and the classes I attended at The Complete Cook and The Cook's Mart. It amazes me, looking back, that everyone wanted to learn how to bake a baguette, pain de mie, and brioche. I would certainly have trouble selling those skills today!

"Other popular classes were fish cookery, herb cookery, and soups," Bullwinkel added. "We would make field trips to a fish wholesaler to look at really fresh fish. I would begin my herb classes in the garden, and we would smell and compare fresh and dried herbs. Students did not seem shocked to see me roast 10 pounds of bones and meat for a brown stock."

Elaine González, an accomplished teacher of "all things chocolate," also often taught at local cookware shops. She later wrote two books on the subject,

became a master chocolatier, started a chocolate consulting firm called Chocolate Artistry, and was voted into the Candy Hall of Fame.

"I was there when the chocolate craze hit this country in the late 1970s and early 1980s," González said. "For me, it all started when The Complete Cook called to say they were looking for someone to substitute-teach a chocolate class during their opening week festivities. I confessed to knowing next to nothing about working with chocolate, but they were so desperate they didn't care. So, using skills from my party-food and cake-decorating experiences, I taught what turned out to be my first class in chocolate artistry: edible, chocolate-mint-flavored place cards, personalized lollipops, and a few fancy confections. Nobody had ever seen anything like that before and neither had I. I must have had an angel sitting on my shoulder that night because in spite of my lack of chocolate experience, everything worked and the excitement in the classroom was beyond description—mine as well as theirs."

Her first book, *Chocolate Artistry,* debuted in 1983 and caught the chocolate wave as it began. "This was the era of the chocolate festivals," González explained. "These weekend getaways were nothing short of chocolate-eating extravaganzas. It was the perfect format for me to teach my techniques, and I became the unofficial queen of the chocolate festivals. The chocolate flowed at those festivals, and the participants devoured every chocolate thing in sight—from the sublime to the ridiculous. I was there when they dunked the cast of *Miami Vice* into a vat of chocolate, when a woman won her weight in chocolate for having submitted the best chocolate recipe, and when a gentleman actually grabbed my chocolate-coated hand and licked it!"

The State Street department store Carson Pirie Scott also got into the cooking school business by beefing up its cookware department and building a demonstration kitchen. The store's director of culinary events, Judith Dunbar Hines, taught basic skills classes and also brought in celebrities on book signing tours or to teach a series of classes. Eventually, Hines was promoted and eventually oversaw 32 stores in the region.

"It was a great way to sharpen my teaching skills," Hines said, "as I had to figure out topical things to teach, such as National Artichoke Day or the first day of winter. Next, I had to figure out what could be demonstrated in 40 minutes and served easily ... I was doing this for an audience of 50 people every day with no assistance.

"Then, Carson's decided it was so timely and successful that it wanted to do this in more of its stores—not just the downtown location. I helped design six more kitchens in stores around the area, and some in Milwaukee and Iowa. The day we opened the last of these new kitchens—with razzmatazz, and well-publicized extensive class schedules—Carson's was sold to a new owner that decided to close all of the kitchens and make them into stockrooms."

Cookware also had become part of the Crate & Barrel retail mix. Gordon Segal and his wife, Carole (a founding Les Dames member) had opened a small store in Old Town in 1962. By the early '80s, it had become one of Chicago's most popular casual home "lifestyle" stores. Their inventory also included

kitchen tools, tabletop items, and eventually, furniture. In 1983, they built a new warehouse in Northbrook and began expanding to locations around the country. By the mid-'90s, sales had grown to $300 million in 46 stores nationwide.

"One of the gourmet items we ordered for the first store was copper cookware from France," Carole remembers. "It arrived in a gorgeous tall wood barrel—about 4 feet tall. So we used it as a prop. Then the items from Sweden came in these crates of beautiful birch wood. They were too good to throw out, so we used them as fixtures, too. We really didn't have a name for the store until a week before we opened. One day, I was downstairs working and a woman walking by stopped and came inside. She asked me what we were planning to name the store. I said I didn't know. The woman—who worked for Hallmark—asked me what we were selling. I said we were selling things that came in barrels and crates. She suggested calling the store Barrel and Crate. I went upstairs to tell Gordon her idea, but told him I liked Crate and Barrel better. Gordon agreed."

For professional culinary training in the '80s, only a handful of schools offered the basics, including the city-run Washburne Trade School on the Southwest Side. Glenview's Père L'Ecole de la Cuisine Française offered classes by chef John Snowden for serious home cooks and aspiring professionals, including a young Sarah Stegner.

Linda Calafiore had the idea that culinary education could be a profitable business. In 1983, she opened a small school she dubbed The Cooking and Hospitality Institute of Chicago (CHIC) in the basement of a Streeterville pub. It became one of the area's largest culinary schools in its new digs on Chestnut Street.

A lingering recession in the early '80s, however, caused problems for many of Chicago's cookware businesses. Nationally, unemployment had reached 10.8 percent, according to Traeger in *The Food Chronology*—the highest unemployment rate since 1940. Many of Chicago's cookware shops and cooking schools struggled. Cooking classes no longer drew large audiences.

As the 1990s began, though, interest in food, cooking, and the requisite pots and pans returned. Consumers wanted the newest coffeemakers and the most professional stockpots. Chain stores offering kitchenware and classes arrived in Chicago, including Sur La Table on Walton Street and Williams-Sonoma in various locations around the city. The Calphalon Company opened a large state-of-the-art demonstration kitchen west of the Loop with a variety of cooking classes. Marshall Field's (now Macy's) on State Street built a state-of-the-art kitchen and classroom near the seventh-floor gourmet-food department and called it the Culinary Studio. Wilton, the cake decorating firm, expanded its cooking class schedules to different venues in the area.

A new generation of noncooks was ready to learn what their mothers hadn't taught them—mostly the basics. Independent cooking schools popped up all over the area. In 1989, Kristen James and Carolynn Friedman opened Prairie Kitchens in the north suburbs; there, they taught classical techniques and recipes using fresh, seasonal ingredients. (James later left the school to open a law practice for small food

businesses.) Another school, The Chopping Block, began in a house in Lincoln Park; owner Shelly Young expanded to two other locations, one of which was much more spacious—the Merchandise Mart. The Wooden Spoon opened in Andersonville, and Corner Cooks continued to thrive in Libertyville.

In the new millennium, many considered cooking classes to be entertainment. Groups of students would take a class as a social evening out, and some would hire a teacher or personal chef to teach them and their friends in a party atmosphere. Cooking classes for singles and couples became popular weekend activities. Corporate groups hired cooking schools to organize evenings of cooking as team-building exercises.

Meal-preparation businesses became a big trend. Students cooked a week's worth of menus for their families with an instructor's direction and help; Bespoke Cuisine and Dinner by Design were two companies that offered such services.

For some, hiring a personal chef was the way to go. (The Personal Chefs Association of America was founded in 1999.) A day's worth of cooking could provide a family with chef-prepared meals for an entire week!

In one of the most telling signs of the new appeal of cooking, more professional cooking schools opened than ever before in Chicago and nationwide. Young people were ready to follow in the footsteps of TV-star chefs and find careers in restaurant kitchens. Culinary schools received more respect than previously—and they began to have long waiting lists of students. The venerable Culinary Institute of America in Hyde Park, New York, opened a branch in the Napa Valley. Johnson & Wales in Providence, Rhode Island, expanded into Florida and North Carolina.

Chicago's culinary educational opportunities kept growing. By the turn of the century, Chicago boasted 14 professional culinary programs in the Chicago area. CHIC's enrollment soared, which led to further expansion at the Chestnut Street location. In 2000, Calafiore sold the school to the Career Education Corporation, a private post-secondary education firm, and the school was invited to become part of the Cordon Bleu of Paris affiliates when the respected cooking school expanded into the United States. Kendall College's Culinary School in Evanston outgrew its space, and in 2005, the school moved to a new city location with cutting-edge teaching kitchens and an elegant student-staffed restaurant.

In addition to CHIC and Kendall, Chicago's culinary schools included the French Pastry School, Lexington College, Robert Morris College's Institute of Culinary Arts, the Illinois Institute of Art, and the Washburne Culinary Institute. In the suburbs, the culinary programs at numerous junior and community colleges experienced growing enrollments.

CULINARY ARTS

The city of Chicago also got into the game—and hired Judith Dunbar Hines as its new director of culinary arts and events. She coordinated and created culinary events with sister cities around the world, and instigated neighborhood food tours, cooking competitions, and seminars. She also began a program of cooking classes for high-school students and the public at Randolph Street's Gallery 37. The job

came about, she said, because of a conference of food professionals in Chicago in 1997.

"The International Association of Culinary Professionals was planning its 18th annual conference in Chicago, and I was asked to be the chairperson," Hines related. "I had been a member and attended all its conferences, and I knew one thing for sure: every conference in every city had memorable parts, but I couldn't remember what city they had been in. So my declared focus for 1997 was that people would go away from the conference with a clear image of Chicago in their minds. That would entail getting out of the hotel as often as possible to see and experience the city, use the stories of Chicago's food history to give them a sense of place, and give the attendees as many real Chicago experiences as possible. So I went first to the Office of Tourism to see what resources they had, and someone there worked with me closely to plan events and tours, and create ideas that would realize my goals.

"When the conference was over, I was asked to see the commissioner of Cultural Affairs I didn't realize that she had visited the conference with the director of the Office of Tourism to see what I'd done.

"When I first came to work for the city, the commissioner said, 'What should we call your job?' I suggested director of culinary events, based on my job at Carson's. She said, 'Well, we are the department of cultural *arts*, so I think it should have art in it.' I brought her a quote from Julia Child that said, 'Cooking is an art of the highest form, and I think people should recognize that.'

"Therefore, my title became director of culinary arts and events. It has evolved into a lot of different types of things, but mostly it is about using the culinary arts to attract tourists to Chicago and give them a better idea of what this city is all about."

Cooking schools and city events were not the only ways to learn about food in Chicago. Several organizations in Chicago provided social and educational opportunities for people interested in food. The Culinary Historians, a group that was started in the early '90s by Roosevelt University history professor Bruce Kraig and others, met weekly to discuss the cultural and historical aspects of food. Other national groups formed local chapters, including the Women Chefs and Restaurateurs, the Roundtable for Women in Foodservice, and Slow Food, an Italy-based organization promoting traditional foods. Restaurant enthusiast Don Newcomb started ChicaGourmets, a dining group with an educational focus.

The boom in computer literacy created another avenue for food information. Online food websites, chats, and forums, like Chowhounds and E-Gullet, became popular ways for food lovers to communicate. Dana Benigno began Chicagocooks.com, a website that features local events, resources and recipes. A Chicago group of Chowhounds formed its own online site, LTH Forum, and held various events and dinners at ethnic restaurants. It seemed as if everyone was talking about food: on the Internet, in meeting halls, and in restaurants.

TO MARKET, TO MARKET

Shopping for food in Chicago has changed as our eating patterns have evolved during the last 25 years. In the early 1980s, cooks everywhere were pinching pennies and clipping coupons, and supermarkets ran on tight profit margins. In 1982, the Great Atlantic & Pacific Tea Co. decided to close all A&P stores in Chicago, Kansas City, and Louisville, according to Traeger in *The Food Chronology*, and Kroger had pulled out of Chicago a few years before. Only Jewel Food Stores and Dominick's Finer Foods remained as major supermarkets in Chicago. Gradually, Dominick's, which was owned by the DiMatteo family, began expanding. Small independent stores filled some of the vacancies left by the chains. The small Treasure Island chain featured stores that were hybrids of regular supermarkets and European-style gourmet stores; its expansive ethnic aisles were a supermarket rarity. Sunset Foods, another small chain in the northern suburbs, took pride in its quality foods and customer service.

Jane Armstrong, a founding member of Les Dames and a retired vice-president for consumer affairs at Jewel, observed many changes in the industry. According to Armstrong, at the beginning of the decade, "people ate at home and cooked from scratch, for the most part." Accordingly, supermarket meat cases were quite long and full, with a greater proportion of large cuts than we see today. Because shoppers generally stuck with beef, pork, and poultry, few stores featured fresh fish. Choices in the produce aisles, bakery, or deli departments included little more than basic all-American selections.

Three factors began to change our supermarkets, according to Armstrong. "People were traveling more, and they had new food experiences that they enjoyed and wanted to continue at home." Slowly, grocery stores began to develop cheese departments, in-store

VEGETABLE FRESCA

This was one of the first salads Convito Italiano carried. I invented it literally out of what was left in the refrigerator that day. Our first tiny shop in Wilmette had no walk-ins—just one little refrigerator. To this day, this salad is a customer favorite.

— Nancy Brussat Barocci

2 cups julienned carrots (2 inches long)	VINAIGRETTE:
2 cups julienned zucchini	½ cup olive oil
1 cup peapods, trimmed	¼ cup red wine vinegar
1 cup peeled, seeded, julienned cucumbers	1 teaspoon salt
1 cup cherry tomatoes, halved	½ teaspoon dried basil
1 small red onion, thinly sliced	⅛ teaspoon dried oregano
2 tablespoons chopped fresh parsley	Freshly ground black pepper

Combine the vegetables and parsley in large bowl. For the vinaigrette, combine the oil, vinegar, salt, basil, oregano, and pepper in medium bowl; whisk to combine. Pour over the vegetables; mix well.

Makes 10 servings.

---

bakeries, and ethnic aisles, and they expanded their deli sections.

As the decade advanced, "more women worked outside the home and had less time to do meal planning and cooking," Armstrong said. As a result, grocery stores and free-standing delicatessens offered more prepared salads and entrees. Food companies began to develop a wider variety of frozen prepared entrées.

Interest in better nutrition also became a factor as people sought ways to reduce their consumption of fat, sodium, calories, and other nutritional no-nos. Supermarkets responded by expanding their produce departments, in-store salad bars, and fresh fish counters.

For fancier fare, Chicagoans had only a few choices. Stop and Shop, a gourmet food shop in the Loop, was one of the few places to find unusual imported foods. According to editors Burton Wolf and William Rice in the 1979 edition of *Where to Eat in America*, it was a "gourmet gallimaufry," where one could find partridge, quail eggs, truffles, and expensive glazed fruits.

Kuhn's and Meyer's Delicatessens offered German and other European goods up on North Lincoln Avenue. Conte Di Savoia, located south of the Loop, was the place to go for dried herbs and spices, more than 40 types of pasta, and tinned imports from all over the world. The store later moved to smaller digs on Taylor Street.

On the North Shore, Convito Italiano was a fresh, modern version of an Italian market. A small gourmet shop specializing in Italian food and wine, it opened in Wilmette in 1980. Owner Nancy Brussat Barocci and her partners were pioneers in a culinary wilderness; this was a time when most people's idea of "take-away" food was either a bucket of deep-fried chicken or a pepperoni pizza, and the great Italian explosion had yet to make its way to the Midwest. Barocci's tiny shop introduced a galaxy of authentic imported Italian food: specialty cheeses and meats in the deli, choice Italian grocery products on the shelves, and freshly prepared homemade salads and pasta sauces for take-out. By 1982, Convito outgrew its 1,500 square foot shop, moved to a space four times larger in nearby Plaza del Lago, expanded its selections and added a café.

Ten years later, Barocci decided to open a French bistro, Betise, across the parking lot from the shop. Her daughter, Candace Barocci Warner, joined the operation in 1996 and later also joined Chicago's Les Dames chapter. When she learned that the Convito building would be torn down in 2007, Barocci combined the two businesses in the Betise space and called it Convito Café & Market.

In 1979, a gourmet take-out shop called Foodstuffs opened in Glencoe, backed by Carole and Gordon Segal of Crate & Barrel. High quality, natural ingredients went into the prepared dishes and desserts made on the premises; shelves were lined with packaged olive oils, vinegars, and imported foods. It eventually expanded to four locations in the northern suburbs. Specialty chains, such as The Home Economist chain, opened stores featuring bulk nuts, dried fruits, and grains. This proved to be some competition for supermarkets, which began adding their own bulk-food departments.

As consumers sought fresher produce, cities began to promote farmers' markets. New York has its Greenmarkets; Seattle has its Pike Place. Chicago was slow to join the group, but as time went on, neighborhood markets began to flourish. "Through the '90s, there was an increasing awareness in how the environment factored into our food," said Mary

Abbott Hess. "There was a definite movement away from the 'me' generation and toward the idea of protecting the world for our children. People thought about eating locally, buying from farmers' markets, and actually knowing your farmer. Although talk of sustainability didn't really emerge until 2000, the movement started well before that."

Abby Mandel founded Chicago's Green City Market in 1998, with Sarah Stegner and Linda Calafiore on its steering committee. The Market's mission was "to improve the availability of a diverse range of high quality foods, to connect local producers and farmers to chefs, restaurateurs, food organizations, and the public, and to support small family farms and promote a healthier society through education and appreciation for local, fresh, sustainably raised produce and products."

The Market grew over the years, eventually featuring produce from about 20 farmers. More chefs frequented the Market. Demonstrations, workshops, and children's classes were added to the Market, which was located in a bucolic setting at the south end of Lincoln Park. Mariana Coyne became the Market's farm "forager"—a role she also held for the City of Chicago farmers markets.

For the first three years of the market, the Les Dames chapter supported the Market through donations of time and money. In 2003, members came up with the idea of a summer barbecue fundraiser for the Market. The group invited area chefs to participate, including Les Dames members Carolyn Collins of Collins Caviar, Judy Contino of Bittersweet Bakery, Pamela Fitzpatrick of Fox & Obel, Gale Gand of Tru, Della Gossett of Charlie Trotter's, Rita Gutekanst of

Limelight Catering, Carrie Nahabedian of NAHA, Ina Pinkney of Ina's, Debra Sharpe of Feast, Sofia Solomon of Tekla, Sarah Stegner of Prairie Grass Café and more. Hundreds of foodies convened at the Market to watch the chefs grill, sample their specialties, and sip wine and beer.

Organics, sustainable farming, and eating locally produced foods became common buzzwords with consumers (and chefs). They began to look for alternatives to Chicago supermarkets. Several organic farmers in the region noticed the trend and joined the community-supported agriculture (CSA) movement by supplying "shares" to consumers. By buying shares, families could purchase a proportion of the farm's crop each season and get deliveries of fresh produce from the farm through the summer and fall. Farmers avoided the use of middlemen, and consumers ate fresher foods. John Peterson's Angelic Organics in Caledonia became one of the first farms to use the CSA model.

Supermarkets also were continuing to change. Supercenters, big-box stores, and food clubs such as Wal-Mart, Super Target, Cub Foods, Sam's Club, Costco, and others began to appear in the city of Chicago and its suburbs. Part-department store and part-supermarket, these huge stores drew shoppers away from regular grocery stores in the mid-'90s. "One-stop" shopping saved them time and gasoline.

By the turn of the century, the variety of foods available in area supermarkets ballooned. Snack aisles offered many new brands of cookies, potato and tortilla chips, and crackers. The soda aisle expanded to include countless new brands of bottled waters, ener-gy drinks, and other "lifestyle" beverages.

As competition heated up, Jewel Food Stores, Dominick's, and other local grocery stores came up with more ways to keep shoppers coming back. They added prepared meats ready to hit the skillet, pre-marinated meats, kebabs, stuffed chops and poultry, and other quick-to-cook items.

The term "home meal replacement" entered the lexicon. In a 1998 report, the trade journal *New Product News* predicted that home meal replacement would soon "fill the need for quick, home-style food as people make less time to cook. Boston Market started the trend in the late '80s by offering whole chicken dinners with all the fixings as takeout food. Now grocery stores are expanding the concept."

The West Coast's HomeGrocer.com and the Midwest's Peapod were two of the first online grocery firms. Their unique order and delivery systems took much of the drudgery out of shopping. Soon, other companies in major urban centers entered the new home-delivery grocery business.

The supermarket landscape also changed again with the 1993 arrival of Whole Foods, which was followed by Fresh Fields, People's Market, and Wild Oats. These stores offered expansive selections of natural and organic foods and foods for special diets, such as vegetarian, lactose-intolerant, and diabetic. In the '60s, '70s, and '80s, the market for these products was primarily served by small independent health food stores, but the arrival of these specialty stores heralded a change for all grocery purveyors. Most supermarkets added small areas of organic produce or packaged goods.

In 2002, the USDA implemented its National

Organics Standards. By 2005, even the giant Wal-Mart chain announced a commitment to organic foods in all of its stores—a move decried by some who believed large organic operations defeated the principles of local, sustainable farming.

The California-based Trader Joe's chain took shopping to a different place, providing low-priced, convenient foods under its own brand name and an extensive selection of value-priced wines. Trader Joe's quickly became the place to go for "something different" in Chicago.

PURVEYORS OF FINE FOODS

Smaller fine-food purveyors also began to blossom in the '90s. When Sam's Wines & Liquors moved to its new location in the city, owner Fred Rosen added a gourmet market within the store, called Marcey Street Market. Its manager, Reysa Samuels, stocked the small shop with a sophisticated selection of imported and American cheeses, cured meats, and packaged gourmet foods to complement the huge stock of wines at Sam's.

In 1992, Judy Contino, the former pastry chef for Ambria restaurant, opened the Bittersweet Pastry Shop on Belmont Avenue, which specializes in intricate tarts, cookies, and wedding cakes. Contino soon expanded, adding a small café that offered light lunches. Today, many more excellent high-end bakeries can be found all over the city, from Pilsen's Bombon Bakery to Clybourn Avenue's Vanille Patisserie.

In 1997, The Spice House opened in Evanston; later, a location in Old Town followed. Owner Patty Erd purchased the business from her parents, who had begun the famous Penzey's spice business in Mil-

waukee. Erd and her husband, Tom, sell herbs and spices from around the world, including customized spice blends mixed on the premises. The Spice House is celebrating 50 years in business in 2007.

In 2001, another new store arrived with some buzz and excitement among area gourmet cooks: Fox & Obel, a high-end urban market similar to New York City's famous Dean & Deluca and Balducci's markets. Fox & Obel stocked gourmet packaged products, fresh prime meats, seafood, unusual produce, artisan breads baked on the premises, desserts, wine, flowers, and prepared, ready-to-go foods. Meme Hopmayer and her husband Gary (who together had started The Great American Scone Co. years before) became founding partners of Fox & Obel. "We started this market because every time we returned from a trip, we yearned for the great markets we saw in other cities," says Hopmayer.

The mix of products and the freshly prepared dishes from the store's small café drew residents and office workers from surrounding River East condos and office towers.

Debra Sharpe opened Bucktown and Gold Coast locations of The Goddess and the Grocer, which offers prepared foods and imported packaged products. Sharpe got her start as a caterer for rock stars such as Axl Rose and Paul McCartney. One of Sharpe's most memorable catering jobs was in 1989, when she was appointed caterer for the Moscow Music Peace Festival at Lenin Stadium. Bon Jovi, Motley Crue, Ozzy Osborne, and many others were playing. Later, Sharpe moved to Chicago and opened spots such as Feast, Half and Half, and Cru Café and Wine Bar.

THE ORIGINAL AMERICAN SCONE

My husband Gary and I started baking scones in the basement of our home in 1987. It was a hobby that grew into a business. In 1988, we opened a bakery that served 13 varieties of scones and coffee, but there was no foot traffic and no parking. After plugging along for a year or so, Jill Van Cleave told us that there was a new coffee shop in town, Starbucks. Starbucks had just opened its third store in Chicago when we became a supplier to the chain. We grew from a small retail bakery into a wholesale scone manufacturer with 100 employees—in many ways because of our relationship with Starbucks. Even when we supplied scones, muffins, and cookies to Starbucks locations in 10 different cities, we continued to make our products by hand. We sold the business in 1998 to start Fox & Obel Market.

—Meme Hopmayer

4	cups all-purpose flour	3	large eggs
3	tablespoons light brown sugar	2	egg yolks
1	tablespoon baking powder	1⅓	cups heavy (whipping) cream
½	teaspoon salt	2	cups (8 ounces) dried currants
6	tablespoons butter, cut into small pieces	1	egg yolk mixed with 1 tablespoon milk or cream for egg wash

Mix together the flour, brown sugar, baking powder, and salt in the large bowl of an electric mixer fitted with the paddle attachment. Add the butter and mix into a flour mixture that resembles coarse meal. Mix together the eggs, yolks, and cream in medium bowl. Add to the dry ingredients and mix just until blended. Do not overmix.

Turn the dough out onto a lightly floured work surface. Flatten the dough and press the currants into it. Fold the dough and incorporate the currants by pressing them with the heel of your hand. Pat the dough into a flat round about ½- to ¾-inch high. Refrigerate for 1 hour.

Preheat the oven to 400°F. Cut the dough into rounds using a 3-inch biscuit cutter. (The dough may be frozen at this time.) Place the scones on the cookie sheet. Brush with the egg wash. Bake until light golden brown, 12 to 15 minutes. Cool on a wire rack. Serve hot.

Makes 12 scones.

Note
The colder the dough, the better it bakes. We used to bake them from a frozen state.

ETHNIC MARKETS

Ethnic markets across the city's neighborhoods have succeeded for two primary reasons: a continual influx of immigrants and experimentation by cooks of all nationalities with more unusual cuisines. Chinatown, which is located south of the Loop, has added a new mall with shops and restaurants. An Asian enclave at Argyle Street on the North Side has become the place to go for Chinese, Thai, and Vietnamese products. Devon Avenue's legendary melting pot continues; today, the area boasts East Indian, Pakistani, Russian, and Jewish restaurants and food shops—to name a few!

Many Asian immigrant populations have shifted

from the city to the suburbs, driving a few Asian mega-stores, such as Mitsuwa in Arlington Heights and Diho in Westmont, to open in response to the migration. On North Lincoln Avenue, Paulina Market still makes traditional German-style sausages, and on Milwaukee Avenue, Bobak's offers Polish versions on a street still lined with Polish restaurants and businesses.

On a sad note, the famous Maxwell Street Market was forced to move from its site near Halsted Street to make room for the expanding University of Illinois at Chicago campus. The new location is at Canal Street and Roosevelt Road, and it will soon move again, to Des Plaines Avenue near Roosevelt Road. Once, the market bustled with Jewish and African-American vendors selling flea-market goods and hot dogs. Today, it is primarily a Hispanic market, and a fine place to find Mexican street food.

"Maxwell Street Market is so much like Mexico," said Deann Bayless. "The street food there is all Mexican. We send people down there all the time. It's a vibrant market, though totally different from the old Maxwell Street."

A WINE EVOLUTION

In many ways, shopping for wine mimicked the changes in food shopping at the end of the 20th century. Chicagoans' "wine sense" seemed to expand along with their growing sophistication about food. In the early '80s, most simply drank "a glass of chablis," according to Barbara Glunz-Donovan. Jug wines were often the only choice and chardonnay was yet to be discovered. In the 1970s, all serious wine came from France, and buyers had to be convinced to give wine list positions to California. Even after the now-famous 1976 Paris Tasting, where California wines outshone their French counterparts in blind taste tests, it took several years for the American public to take notice. But by 1982, the wine craze had begun. By the mid-'80s, California wines dominated sales, and the Napa Valley became a "destination."

In Chicago, the California boom was reflected on the shelves of the city's many wine retailers. In addition to The House of Glunz, Chicagoans found bottles at places such as Bragno's; Sam's Wine Warehouse; Schaefer's Wines in Skokie; Armanetti's; Gold Standard Liquors; and the Chalet Wine and Cheese Shops.

Consumers who wanted to learn more about wine could take a class at the Chicago Wine School. Owner Patrick Fegan taught basic to advanced classes on varietals, wine regions, and the proper way to taste wine. Many wine lovers joined John Davis's A Taste of California wine club and received monthly shipments of little-known wines. Davis was also the owner of Geja's Café, a fondue restaurant where wine is a very important part of the menu.

"Women—both those working in the wine industry and as consumers—formed a growing segment of wine aficionados," Glunz-Donovan said. She pointed out that in the early '80s, only a few women worked full-time in the industry; in Chicago, notable women in the business included Glunz-Donovan, Myrna Greenspan, Debra Crestoni, and Mary Ross, Chicago's first female sommelier at the Signature Room restaurant at the 95th. By 2007, the wine-industry scene for women had changed dramatically; women now own wineries, wine shops, and distributorships, and many women are winemakers, critics, sommeliers, journalists, and consultants.

Crestoni got her start as a sommelier and later worked with Pete Stern, who owned Connoisseur Wines Ltd. on Chestnut Street. Stern specialized in Burgundies and Rhone wines. Crestoni opened her own importing firm in 1999 and called it Connoisseur Wines, in honor of her mentor. She works with smaller, often little-known wineries, and is one of the few female importers/distributors in the country.

For Italian wines, Nancy Brussat Barocci's Convito Italiano was the place to go. She brought in the world-class and undervalued wines of Antinori, Gaja and Mastroberardino in 1980. Convito became the first wine shop in America to be awarded the coveted Vinarious and Vide Awards for excellence in selection and customer education.

Leonard Solomon's Wines & Spirits, an importer of wines, caviar, and cheeses, was the first firm to bring in little-known Australian vintages, according to his wife, Sofia Solomon. He died in 2002, but Solomon has continued his business, as well as her own importing firm, TEKLA, Inc.

A pursuit of powerful flavors—and reports of health benefits—soon made red wine the top choice of Chicagoans and Americans nationwide (though chardonnay remained a big seller everywhere). Cabernet sauvignon is America's favorite red grape, and pinot noir isn't far behind. "Was it all because of the movie *Sideways*, or perhaps had the nation's taste become more discreet?" Glunz-Donovan asked, referring to the 2005 film in which a leading character spurns merlot in favor of pinot noir. Chardonnay continues to dominate in the white category, although the preferred style is now less-oak, and in some cases completely unoaked, chardonnays.

California was no longer the only region producing great American wine. Myriad new American viticultural areas are achieving recognition, in almost every state in the union. As for the imports, wines from Austria, Australia, South Africa, New Zealand, Chile, and Argentina were rarely seen in Chicago wine shops in the early '80s. By the late '90s, they were everywhere. A new variety of appellations from France, Italy and Spain also appeared. Little-known grapes, such as gruner veltliner, albariño, carmenere, and malbec, made their way to Chicago shelves.

At the dawn of the new millennium, Chicago was one of the top wine markets in the country. Fine wine and spirits shops dot the neighborhoods and suburbs. Local rare-wine auction houses, starting with Heublien in the '70s and leading to the present day's Hart Davis Hart and Kensington's Fine and Rare Wines, draw international attention. Several small distributors, such as Vin Divino, Cream Wine Co., and Crestoni's Connoisseur Wines, augment the inventories of the major houses by offering wines from every appellation around the world plus rare limited-production wines that attract collectors.

Lake Bluff's Terlato Wine Group, an importing and distributing firm, added winemaking to its list of businesses when it purchased several California wineries. Closer to home, a few suburban wineries have won awards for made-on-the-premises bottles. Lynfred Winery in Roselle is the oldest; it was joined later by Fox Valley Winery in Oswego and the Glunz Family Winery in Grayslake.

As Chicagoans became more familiar with wine, wine bars multiplied around the city. The venerable Pops for Champagne moved from Lincoln Park to State

Street and closed its Highwood location. Randolph Street Cellars opened west of the Loop, combining a retail shop with a wine bar. Bin 36 offers a small retail store, a wine bar where patrons can order "flights" of wine, and a full restaurant. Webster's Wine Bar on the North Side and The Stained Glass wine bar in Evanston also draw increasingly sophisticated customers.

Just as Chicagoans have grown to admire the international style of fruit-forward, intensely flavored wines made by "flying winemakers," the move toward organic, terroir-driven wines has captured our attention as well.

Top producers in France began the biodynamic movement in winemaking, which soon found committed followers around the world. Chemical-free biodynamic wines are considered by many to be healthier for the imbiber than "high-tech" wines. Simultaneously, among many serious, educated consumers, the "drink less, but drink better" mentality has prevailed.

Not to be left behind, the artisan beer business grew through the '90s to include local breweries/beer pubs such as Goose Island, Flossmoor Station, Two Brothers, and Flatlander's. All have helped boost Chicago out of its "beer depression." Like wine appreciation, the evolution of beer brewed in Chicago was just another facet of Chicago's changing culinary scene.

Artisan, local, sustainable, quality: These were the buzzwords of the new century in wine, beer, and food.

A FOOD (COMPANY) TOWN

From the beginning, Chicago attracted food manufacturers and related businesses. Its location on the Great Lakes provided access to shipping. Later, the city became an important hub for rail transportation,

and grains such as wheat, corn, and oats grown in the Midwest moved easily through Chicago. Cheese and butter were processed here from milk brought in from upper Midwestern dairy farms. Of course, Chicago's stockyards were the center of the meatpacking industry.

Quaker Oats was one of the early companies to set up shop in Chicago. According to Katherine Smith, who became a vice president of Quaker Oats, Quaker offered public tours of its test kitchens in the Merchandise Mart and nearby Quaker Tower for many years. PepsiCo purchased Quaker in the late 1990s, but Quaker's offices are still located in Chicago's River North neighborhood.

Glenview-based Kraft Foods started in 1903 in Chicago with cheese products, including nationwide bestseller Velveeta. Dorothy Holland spent many years at Kraft as a spokeswoman and director of the Kraft Test Kitchens located near Navy Pier; the company later moved to the northern suburbs. Some products that are well known today and first tested in the Chicago kitchens were Kraft Mayonnaise, Kraft Marshmallows, and Philadelphia Cream Cheese.

The canned-food company Libby, McNeill & Libby also had test kitchens in downtown Chicago for many years. Purchased by Nestlé in the 1970s, the firm was started in 1868 with a focus on canning meat; later, it was purchased by Chicago's Swift & Company, which manufactured meat products, and began to market canned fruits and vegetables, including the famous Libby's Pumpkin Purée—still a classic for Thanksgiving desserts around the nation.

Other meat packers with a significant Chicago presence included Armour, Eckrich, and Oscar

Mayer (now part of Kraft). Food companies that are currently headquartered in the Chicago area include Alberto Culver, NutraSweet, Ferrara Pan Candy, Sara Lee, Fannie Mae Candy, Vienna Beef, Tootsie Roll, Eli's Cheesecake, Dean Foods, Morton Salt and Blommer Chocolate Company.

FEEDING CHICAGO

Not all of the city's food firms are giant corporations. The Flying Food Group started small in 1983, when Sue Ling Gin created it to supply food for Chicago-based Midway Airlines. She soon expanded her operation to other airports around the country, and eventually it served 80 airlines at 9 U.S. airports—until the events of September 11, 2001, devastated the airline business. Forced to regroup, Gin moved into gourmet packaged foods for grocery stores and slowly rebuilt the airline food purveyor segment. Today, her company is one of the largest minority-owned firms in Chicago.

Nicole Bergere is the founder of Nicole's Inc., a firm that supplies quality handmade crackers and other baked goods to retail stores, restaurants, and hotels.

She leased a tiny storefront shop to open her bakeshop in 1984 on Touhy Avenue, far north of downtown Chicago. It was only about 1,000 square feet of space, and she had a business partner and one young helper, she said.

"It started as a retail neighborhood bakeshop serving breads to a residential area of mixed ethnicity," she said. But this "hood" turned out to be a bad location without parking or destination shoppers. She added wholesale sales to her repertoire almost immediately. "I bought whole organic grains and ground them for

the breads." According to Bergere, hers was perhaps the only bakery in the city to grind its own grains.

She pitched Neiman-Marcus to sell her baked goods in their stores, and some of the store's personnel came to Bergere's tiny bakeshop for a tasting—and loved it all. Then, in 1989, after she sold her breads in an American Institute of Wine and Food-sponsored "Best of the Midwest Market," a one-day farmer's market event held on Navy Pier, she impressed representatives from the Ritz-Carlton Chicago; the hotel is still a customer to this day.

By the end of the '80s, Bergere could see that Chicagoans were getting more and more interested in natural products, whole grains, and the taste of unadulterated foods. Her time had arrived. In 1994, Nicole moved her bakeshop—now focused on wholesale accounts—to a warehouse of spacious proportions on Kingsbury Street, south of North Avenue. It was here that she launched her popular Nicole's Divine Crackers.

Carolyn Collins started an unlikely business for the Midwest—a caviar company, Collins Caviar; she uses the roe from Lake Michigan fish to create a variety of plain and flavored caviars.

"I loved fishing in our local gravel pits stocked with perch, bluegills, and bass, or trolling for salmon from a boat on Lake Michigan," Collins said. "In the fall, mature Chinook would yield sacs of eggs that weighed 3 to 5 pounds. I couldn't bear to throw away those beauties, so I taught myself a hand-cleaning technique and started to make salmon roe caviar as a hobby. A chef-friend discovered this hobby and put the caviar on his menu as an exclusive for his new restaurant."

Collins Caviar is the only American company that

actually processes caviar, she added. The line includes flavored and smoked caviars, and all the products are from freshwater fish.

Camilla Nielson took over her husband's firm, Nielson-Massey Vanillas Inc. of Waukegan, after his death. Nielson-Massey manufactures vanilla, and Nielson has become a traveling ambassador for the product.

Frontera Foods, Inc. was started in 1996, when former Kraft executive Manny Valdes and JeanMarie Brownson partnered with the Baylesses. Today, Frontera Foods is the premier Mexican specialty-food company in the country, offering more than 60 gourmet Mexican food products, including salsas, chips, and pizzas.

ADVOCATING, MARKETING, AND SUPPORTING THE FOOD INDUSTRY IN CHICAGO

With such an abundance of food firms in the area, it was only a matter of time before food trade associations also located here; they included the American Dairy Association in Rosemont, the National Live Stock and Meat Board (later, the National Cattlemen's Beef Association), and the Supermarket Institute (later the Food Marketing Institute, now located in Washington, D.C.) The Wisconsin Milk Marketing Board set up a main office in the Chicago area; there, Marilyn Wilkinson helps promote Wisconsin cheeses as Director of National Products Communications.

Food advertising and marketing public relations were and continue to be major forces in Chicago. Chicago-based Leo Burnett was an early communica-

tions agency and created some of the country's most beloved advertising characters, including the Pillsbury Dough Boy, Tony the Tiger, and the Jolly Green Giant.

In 1981, another major food public relations firm, D. J. Edelman Communications, introduced Swift's enormously popular Butterball Turkey Talk-Line. Nancy Rodriguez, who is now president of her own Oak Park-based business, Food Marketing Support Services, was on board as director for the Talk-Line's first Thanksgiving. Rodriguez remembers, "The concept was designed by Edelman to respond to the annual before-the-feast deluge of calls to Swift's consumer-response team. It was apparent to those of us on the internal [Swift] side that turkey instilled trepidation in the hearts of home cooks. The enormity of educating American home cooks, as well as butchers, chefs, FDA Meat and Poultry Hotline folks, and so on, was daunting. Barbara Molotsky of Edelman had the idea, and I was the internal make-it-happen person. It was a great idea, but a Herculean endeavor to implement. We were incredibly wise but naïve: Wise, because we hired food professionals, trained them extensively in turkey science, preparation techniques, and customized responses, and naïve, because we had no idea what the call volume would be like. Seven operators with only five telephones personally handled 11,000 callers in 6 weeks. We had 22,000 inquiries that first year. AT&T sent a local VP to find out what was going on in Oak Brook, since its entire Hinsdale substation was overwhelmed. We made lots of upgrades and improvements over the years, and it has been successful beyond our dreams."

Food stylists, consultants, and recipe developers became integral to the food marketing process by supporting these agencies and food companies. Food consultant Karen Levin, for example, created recipes for food manufacturers and screens many entries for recipe contests. Food stylist Carol Smoler prepared and designed food for print and television advertisements and for many cookbooks.

Marian Tripp was legendary in food public relations. She created the food department at J. Walter Thompson and then founded her own company in 1975, Marian Tripp Communications. One of the founding members of Chicago Les Dames, Tripp represented such clients as the Supermarket Institute, Uncle Ben's Rice, The Quaker Oats Company, and the National Live Stock and Meat Board. Tripp often organized seminars for the press and attracted nationally known speakers, such as Martha Stewart, Wolfgang Puck and Faith Popcorn, to Chicago.

One memorable success was the effort made by Tripp and her staff to promote the small, family-owned Pace Picante Sauce. Eventually, the Pace business grew into a nationally distributed, successful product that later was purchased by the Campbell Soup Company and became a national brand.

Brenda McDowell and Lisa Piasecki-Rosskamm worked with Tripp and later opened their own Chicago firm, McDowell & Piasecki Food Communications, Inc., with clients such as the National Cattlemen's Beef Association.

The acceptance of Chicago today as one of the country's prime culinary destinations can be traced to the vision and hard work of a remarkable cast of culinary characters such as Tripp, Elaine Sherman, and many more who were at the forefront of change. First-class dining, food and wine retailers and wholesalers, producers, and teachers—Chicago has them all. The city's remarkable evolution from "cowtown" to a sophisticated culinary capital deserves a nod from all who cook or dine here.

GRILLED PORK TENDERLOIN WITH PEACH SALSA AND SPINACH SALAD • *Page 148*

MEXICAN MEATBALLS IN CHIPOTLE-CHILI SAUCE • *Page 154*

CHOCOLATE PECAN CARAMEL TORTE · *Page 34*

CHEESE STICKS • *Page 176*

VEGETABLE FRESCA • *Page 68*

CHOCOLATE BUTTER PECAN TOFFEE · *Page 108*

GARLIC MASHED POTATOES · *Page 171*

OYSTER SAFFRON BISQUE · *Page 180*

SUN-DRIED TOMATO-STUFFED BEEF TENDERLOIN • *Page 182*

ROASTED PEPPER SALAD WITH BASIL AND GOAT CHEESE • *Page 138*

MOROCCAN CHICKEN · *Page 161*

MILE-HIGH FRESH BLUEBERRY PIE • *Page 149*

ONION FLAN • *Page 30*

FETTUCCINE WITH LOBSTER SAUCE • *Page 103*

LEMON SOUFFLÉ CREPES • *Page 118*

SUMMERTIME MARGARITAS • *Page 152*

PART TWO:

MENUS FOR ENTERTAINING

NEW YEAR'S EVE WITH FRIENDS

Bellini Salad*

Freshly Baked Bread

Fettuccine with Lobster Sauce*

Roasted Asparagus with Lemon

Chocolate Mousse Torte*

WINE RECOMMENDATIONS:

White: A brut sparkling wine or Semillon/Sauvignon blend (Bordeaux)

Red: Loire Cabernet Franc or Pinot Noir rosé

BELLINI SALAD

I often serve Insalata Bellini *as a first course followed by a pasta dish. The fresh fruits and vegetables, coupled with toasted almonds and elegant dressing, make this colorful combination perfect for a celebration menu. For an entrée salad, serve with strips of grilled chicken on top or with sautéed or grilled shrimp or calamari. This luscious salad has been on the menu at Convito Italiano during the summer season for many years.*

— Candace Barocci Warner

2	medium peaches, peeled, pitted, *or* 1 bag (8 ounces) frozen peach slices
¼	cup Champagne vinegar
¼	cup olive oil
	Pinch ground ginger
	Salt and white pepper, freshly ground, to taste
8	ounces baby spinach leaves, rinsed, patted dry
1	pint strawberries, hulled, sliced
⅓	cup sliced almonds, toasted
1	tablespoon fresh marjoram leaves

To make the vinaigrette, purée peaches in a food processor until smooth. In a small bowl, whisk the peach purée with Champagne vinegar and olive oil. Add the ginger, salt, and white pepper, to taste.

Place the spinach in a salad bowl with the strawberries, toasted almonds, and fresh marjoram. Toss together with the vinaigrette.

Makes 4 servings.

FETTUCCINE WITH LOBSTER SAUCE

I love to celebrate. I celebrate everything, including the first date I had with my husband, our wedding date, family birthdays, holidays — everything. Champagne always comes to mind when I think of celebrating.

Lobster is one of my favorite foods. My husband and I love to experiment in the kitchen. We have created many different dishes using lobster, and this is one of our favorites.   —*Candace Barocci Warner*

2	fresh whole lobsters, about 1½ lbs. each
	Salt, to taste
¾	cup (1½ sticks) unsalted butter, divided
1	tablespoon olive oil
⅓	cup rum
1	pound dried fettuccine
1	cup chopped onions
2	cloves garlic, minced
5	ripe plum (Roma) tomatoes, peeled, seeded, and roughly chopped
¼ to ⅓ cup heavy (whipping) cream	

To cook the lobsters, heat salted water to a boil in an extra large stockpot or in two separate large saucepans. Add the lobsters to boiling water and cook for approximately 10 minutes. Remove the lobsters with tongs and submerge them in cold water. (Save 2 cups of the cooking water for the next step.)

When the lobsters are cool, place them on a baking sheet. To remove the lobster meat, cut the claws and tail open, and extract the meat. Cut the lobster meat into bite-sized pieces, place them in a bowl, and set aside, covered. Reserve the little claws and vacated shells for stock. Strain and reserve the remaining lobster juices on the baking sheet.

Melt ½ cup of the butter and the olive oil in a large saucepan over medium-low heat. Add the rum. Add 2 cups of the reserved lobster cooking water, the reserved little claws, the shells, and the strained juices. Cover and cook over medium-high heat for 10 minutes. Uncover and boil gently until the liquid has reduced to ¾ cup, about 20 minutes. Allow the reduction to cool and then remove the claws and shells with a slotted spoon. Strain the reduced stock over the reserved lobster meat. Refrigerate for several hours or overnight.

Heat a stockpot of salted water to a boil. Add pasta. Cook according to package directions. Meanwhile, melt the remaining ¼ cup butter in a large skillet over low heat. Add the onions and cook until lightly browned, about 10 minutes. Stir in the garlic and cook for 30 seconds. Add the chopped tomatoes and cook 5 more minutes. Add the stock, lobster meat and cream. Cook for another 2 to 3 minutes. Drain pasta. Toss with lobster sauce in large serving bowl. Serve immediately.

Makes 4 servings.

CHAMPAGNE AND DESSERT WINES

A party is the perfect time for Champagne. Champagne is a tiny region in northern France, where a combination of climate, soil, and grapes creates a truly unique wine. Next, a highly regulated method transforms the wine into a sparkling wine. This method, and several others, are used to produce sparkling wines around the world, but the name "Champagne" is protected by the European Union and respected by almost all producers. Other sparkling wines include Franciacorta and Asti (Italy), Cava (Spain), Sekt (Germany), Blanquette de Limoux and Crémant (France), or simply "sparkling wine" (United States, Australia, and South Africa).

Dessert wines, with their many styles and flavors, can be paired with food or can be served as a dessert itself with nuts and dried fruit or simple cookies. Fortified wines, including Port, Sherry, Madeira, and Marsala, range from very dry to quite sweet, and they have varied uses in the kitchen and in the dining room. France's Vin Doux Naturale is also fortified with alcohol to retain sugar. Banyuls is often paired with chocolate, and Muscat is superb with stone fruits. Italy's Vin Santo and Hungary's Tokaji are other examples.

Another type of sweet wine is produced from grapes infected with Botrytis, which is also called the "noble rot." The king of sweet wines is Bordeaux's Sauternes, and Germany's Beerenauslese and Trockenbeerenauslese yield a unique, sweet flavor. Late-harvest wines, which are made from grapes left on the vine to dry in order to increase their sugar content, also are worth trying.

STORAGE TIPS

Any cool, dark closet or space void of abrupt temperature changes will do. Do not keep wines—particularly sparkling wines—in the refrigerator for weeks. Opened bottles will keep for a few days under refrigeration if the airspace is filled with an inert gas. Better yet, keep a clean, empty half-bottle for any remainder wine. Fill it to the top and cork it.

WINE GLASSES

From Crate and Barrel to Baccarat, the options in wine glasses are endless. Crystal companies want us to believe that we must have the "right" glass for each different grape, which of course means you'll be needing a new cabinet! Truthfully, the matter can be simplified. For everyday enjoyment, choose a clear, well-balanced glass that has space to swirl the wine for aromatic enjoyment, a stem to keep greasy prints from obscuring the wine's clarity, and a price that allows replacement without drama. Crystal, rather than glass, is preferred. You will notice the difference. For multiwine dinners, an upright and slender white-wine glass and a bigger-bowled red-wine glass are quite sufficient to please you and your guests.

—Barbara Glunz-Donovan

CHOCOLATE MOUSSE TORTE

I have made this dish for more than 20 years and, as such, it is one of my favorites. This rich celebration of chocolate can be varied according to your personal taste, as noted in the recipe suggestions. Enjoy this luscious dessert any time of the year.   *— Jennifer Anderson*

        1½ cups chocolate wafer crumbs
        6   tablespoons unsalted butter, melted
        1½ cups heavy (whipping) cream
             Dash of espresso powder
        1   package (12 ounces) semi-sweet chocolate chips
        5   egg yolks
        3   tablespoons brandy, rum, *or* other favorite liquor

Combine the crumbs and melted butter in a small bowl; mix well. Evenly pat the crumb mixture over the bottom and up the sides of a 7-inch springform pan. Refrigerate.

In a small saucepan, heat the cream and espresso powder just to a boil. Meanwhile, combine the chocolate chips, egg yolks, and brandy in a food processor or blender. With the motor running, slowly add the hot cream to the chocolate mixture. Blend 1 minute. Pour into the prepared crust. Refrigerate at least 6 hours. Carefully remove the sides of the pan before serving.

Makes 12 servings.

Notes

This holds well in the refrigerator for up to 1 week.

Grated lemon or orange rind (colored part only) may be added to filling.

Mint chocolate chips may be substituted for chocolate chips.

VALENTINE'S DAY DESSERT BUFFET

Chocolate Butter Pecan Toffee*

Spicy Ginger Cookies*

Graham Cracker Cake*

Biscotti with Cocoa Nibs*

Decadent Chocolate Hazelnut Cake*

WINE RECOMMENDATIONS:

Moscato d'Asti or other light bodied, off-dry sparkling wine

CHOCOLATE BUTTER PECAN TOFFEE

This is my very special recipe for English toffee. It is adapted from my book, The Art of Chocolate *(Chronicle Books).*

— *Elaine González*

> 1½ pounds pecans, coarsely chopped
> 1   cup (2 sticks) unsalted butter, cut into chunks
> 1¼ cups granulated sugar
> ⅓   cup hot water
> 1   pound milk chocolate, coarsely chopped

Grease an inverted 18-by-12-inch baking sheet (or a marble/granite surface) with vegetable oil. Have on hand a candy thermometer, a long wooden spoon, an angled metal spatula, waxed paper, a 10-inch pie plate, a pair of latex gloves (available in most drugstores), and several large sided baking sheets. Place the pecans in another baking sheet.

Combine the butter, sugar, and hot water in a heavy 3-quart saucepan, stirring to blend well. Cook over medium-high heat, stirring occasionally, until the mixture comes to a boil. Continue to cook and stir until the temperature reaches 300°F on the candy thermometer, about 10 minutes.

Pour the hot mixture on the greased prepared baking sheet in an oblong pool (do not scrape saucepan clean). Use the angled spatula to spread the hot mixture evenly over most of the surface. Slide the spatula under the toffee to loosen it from baking sheet as it cools. When it is cool enough to handle, break the toffee into irregular-sized pieces and layer them between sheets of waxed paper on a baking sheet.

Place the toffee pieces to your left, the pie plate in the center, and the chopped pecans to your right, with another baking sheet behind it (reverse the order if you're left-handed).

Melt the chocolate in the top of a double boiler over hot (but not boiling) water or in microwave oven on high for about 2 minutes, stirring occasionally. Pour into pie plate.

With gloved hands, smear both sides of each toffee piece with chocolate. Place in a bed of pecans, quickly covering each piece with nuts before the chocolate dries. Stack the finished pieces in layers on baking sheet. Refrigerate until the chocolate sets, about 20 minutes.

Store in an airtight container at room temperature for up to 1 month (under lock and key).

Makes about 2½ pounds.

SPICY GINGER COOKIES

When The Spice House first decided to add a recipe section to our website, we invited our customers to send us their tried-and-true recipes, using spices, of course.

Much to our surprise, two out of every three recipes that came in featured ginger. What would make ginger the spice of choice⁄ After giving it some serious thought, we realized this was not so surprising. Ginger, one of the "master spices," holds a very important role in the history of spices. At certain periods in time, it was considered the most important of all spices, and in many countries, roads that housed the spice merchant shops were known as Ginger Street or Ginger Row.

Ginger is a rare spice in that its culinary usage favors savory dishes as well as sweet. In the long history of Asian cuisine, ginger plays a yang, or warming role, to counterbalance the cooling yin. Ginger also has a preservative quality. The well-known Elizabethan herbalist Nicholas Culpeper noted another important property of ginger—he prescribed it to female patients who were "weak in the sports of Venus!"

These cookies can be made ahead of time and frozen, and they store well at room temperature for a week in an airtight container.

— Patty Erd

2 cups all-purpose flour	½ cup vegetable shortening
2½ teaspoons ground ginger	¼ cup (½ stick) unsalted butter, softened
2 teaspoons baking soda	1 cup packed light brown sugar
1 teaspoon ground cinnamon	1 egg
1 teaspoon ground cloves	¼ cup dark molasses
¾ teaspoon salt	1 teaspoon fresh ginger juice (optional)
¾ cup candied/crystallized ginger, cut into minced-size pieces, or ginger nibs	Ginger sugar, or granulated sugar, for rolling

Combine the flour, ground ginger, baking soda, cinnamon, cloves, and salt in medium bowl. Mix together and add the candied ginger.

Cream the vegetable shortening and butter with light brown sugar. Add the egg and molasses. Mix well. Add the fresh ginger juice, if desired. Stir in dry flour mixture. Do not overmix. Cover and chill for 1 hour.

Preheat the oven to 350°F. Form the dough into 1¼- to 1½-inch balls, or use a melon baller to make bite-sized cookies. Roll the cookie dough balls in ginger sugar or granulated sugar. Place on an ungreased baking sheet about 2 inches apart. Bake until set, 12 to 14 minutes. Cool on baking sheet 1 minute, then transfer to wire racks to cool. The cookies will crack on top while baking (as good ginger snaps should).

Makes about 2 to 3 dozen cookies.

Notes

Ginger nibs are crystallized ginger pieces that are sized ¼-inch or smaller.

If you ever buy bags of crystallized ginger, there is always some sugar left at the bottom of the bag—this is what we used to coat our cookies. You can also make your own ginger sugar by mixing 1 teaspoon ground ginger with ¼ cup granulated sugar.

SPICE SAVVY

If you are looking to buy spices, always do so in a shop where you can smell and taste them. Merchants who take pride in the quality of their products should be eager to share their knowledge with you. A good spice merchant can tell you when the ginger was ground, when a batch of curry was mixed, when the new crop of saffron will arrive in the U.S., or which vanilla-bean crop is superior.

The flavors of spices are derived from their essential oils, which are released when they are ground. The moment the oil is released, it begins to dissipate. A good example to crystallize this thought is cinnamon, the bark of a tree. When you grind cinnamon, the essential oil gives you a beautiful, strong, sweet cinnamon flavor. Once this oil is gone, what you have left is sawdust! Placing your spices in an airtight container can prolong the life of the oil, and refrigeration also helps. Mark the date of purchase on your bottles. Think of time and air as enemies of spices!

There are many tried and true food and spice pairings. Allspice is a great ingredient in a barbecue sauce; nutmeg and mace are wonderful, subtle flavor components to add to squash; epazote is a must in Mexican bean dishes; and in Germany, *bonnenkraut*, or summer savory, is the herb of choice for beans. Basil and oregano have an affinity for tomato sauce; coriander and cumin are essential to the cuisines of India, Latin America, southeast Asia, and north Africa, and cumin is also the prima donna of spices in Mexican and Latin-American seasonings.

Salt, of course, is an essential ingredient to all cooking, as it enhances and encourages other flavors to come forward or integrate.

The list goes on and on, but using spices is a truly subjective endeavor. It would be no more authentic to authoritatively advise people which spices to use when cooking a certain dish than it would be for one to tell an artist what medium to work in, or what colors he should choose. Suggestions are all anyone should give you, and whether or not you enjoy the results will vary depending on the genetic makeup of your taste buds. If you suggest that cilantro is necessary for most Mexican cooking, those who find the flavor of cilantro to be soapy probably won't listen.

There is one simple key to unlocking the secret of spices and seasonings that applies to all kitchens and cooks: freshness. While whole spices will keep for at least three years, ground spices are not as sturdy. One year is generally thought to be the rule of thumb for shelf life, although a recent Johns Hopkins study placed the true lifespan of a ground spice at six months.

—Patty Erd

GRAHAM CRACKER CAKE

A favorite family recipe from my mother, this simple, comforting cake becomes even more festive with the fresh berry garnish.

—*Carol Mighton Haddix*

1   cup all-purpose flour
1   cup granulated sugar
3½ teaspoons baking powder
¾ teaspoon salt
2   cups graham cracker crumbs
¾ cup vegetable shortening
1   cup plus 2 tablespoons milk
1½ teaspoons pure vanilla extract
3   large eggs

FILLING:

1½ cups milk
1   vanilla bean, *or* 1½ teaspoons pure vanilla extract
½ cup granulated sugar
¼ cup all-purpose flour
4   beaten egg yolks
    Sweetened whipped cream, *or* buttercream frosting
    Fresh berries for garnish

Preheat the oven to 375°F. Grease and line 2 (9-inch) round cake pans with parchment paper. Sift the flour, sugar, baking powder, and salt into large mixing bowl. Add the graham cracker crumbs, shortening, milk, and vanilla. Beat at a low speed until the crumbs are moistened, then beat 2 minutes at medium speed.

Add the eggs, beating well after each addition. Pour batter into prepared pans. Bake until top springs back when pressed lightly with fingertip, 25 to 30 minutes. Remove from the oven; cool on a wire rack 10 minutes. Remove from pans; cool completely.

For the filling, bring the milk and the vanilla bean almost to a boil in a small saucepan; remove from heat. Combine the sugar, flour, and beaten egg yolks in the top of a double boiler over boiling water. Beat until light. Remove the vanilla bean from the milk and add the milk gradually to the creamed mixture. Stir until well blended. Cook, stirring, until just before mixture reaches the boiling point and thickens. Remove from heat and continue stirring until cool. Cool completely.

To assemble, slice each cake layer in half horizontally. Spread the cooled filling on each layer and stack. Frost the cake with sweetened whipped cream or buttercream frosting. Garnish with fresh berries.

Makes 12 servings.

BISCOTTI WITH COCOA NIBS

I brought this biscotti recipe to a Les Dames holiday party, and it was such a hit that I was asked to send the recipe for inclusion in our quarterly newsletter. — *Madelaine Bullwinkel*

½ cup (1 stick) unsalted butter, at room temperature

⅓ cup granulated sugar

⅓ cup packed dark brown sugar

2 large eggs

1 teaspoon pure vanilla extract

2 cups all-purpose flour

½ tablespoon baking powder

¼ teaspoon sea salt

⅔ cup Marcona almonds, chopped

¼ cup toasted hazelnuts, chopped

⅔ cup chocolate-covered cocoa nibs (such as Scharffen Berger)

1 bar (3½ ounces) high-quality extra dark (70% cacao) chocolate, chopped into ¼-inch pieces (such as Lindt brand)

CHOCOLATE GLAZE:

2 ounces high-quality extra dark (70% cacao) chocolate (such as Lindt brand)

½ tablespoon vegetable oil

Preheat the oven to 325°F. Line a baking sheet with a silicone baking mat or parchment paper. Cream the butter and sugars in the large bowl of an electric mixer until light and fluffy, at least 2 minutes. Beat in eggs, one at a time. Stir in vanilla. Scrape down the sides of the bowl. Sift together the flour and baking powder; add salt. Add the dry ingredients to the butter mixture in three batches, and mix just until blended. Stir the nuts, nibs, and chocolate pieces into the dough until just mixed in.

Turn dough out onto lightly floured work surface. Dust dough with flour and divide in half. Shape dough into logs 2 inches wide by 1 inch high by 12 inches long, and place on prepared baking sheet. Bake until firm and lightly browned, 30 minutes.

Reduce the oven temperature to 300°F. Allow the loaves to cool on wire rack 10 minutes. Lift the loaves onto a cutting board and slice with a serrated knife at a 45-degree angle into ¾-inch-thick slices. Return the slices, cut sides up, to baking sheet. Bake until baked through, 10 to 12 minutes. Remove from the oven; when cool enough to handle, transfer the slices to wire rack to cool.

For the chocolate glaze, break the chocolate into pieces; place in bowl with oil. Microwave on high just until melted, about 1 minute; stir until smooth. Drizzle warm glaze over cooled biscotti. Allow the glaze to set at room temperature.

Makes 2 dozen.

DECADENT CHOCOLATE HAZELNUT CAKE

When my husband and I decided to elope on the eve of the millennium, we didn't have a lot of time to plan anything fancy, but I knew I wanted something really special. I made this cake the day before and we enjoyed it with some fabulously expensive Champagne to commemorate the event. I have made it many times since, and it's always a hit!

— Sara Reddington

1	pound high-quality semi-sweet, or bittersweet, chocolate
1	jar (13 ounces) chocolate hazelnut spread (such as Nutella brand)
¾	cup almond butter
6	large eggs
½	cup granulated sugar
1	cup heavy (whipping) cream

Heat oven to 350°F. Grease a 10-inch springform pan. Wrap heavy-duty foil around outside of pan to make it waterproof.

Coarsely chop chocolate; place in a large glass bowl. Microwave on high 2 minutes; stir until chocolate is melted. Stir in chocolate hazelnut spread and almond butter until smooth. Microwave for additional 30 to 60 seconds if it is difficult to stir.

Beat eggs in the large bowl of an electric mixer until frothy. Gradually add the sugar; continue beating at medium speed until mixture thickens, about 5 minutes. Add the chocolate mixture to the egg mixture, stirring until well combined.

In a separate chilled bowl, beat cream until soft peaks form. Gently fold a large spoonful of whipped cream into the chocolate mixture to lighten it. Gently fold the remaining whipped cream and the chocolate mixture together. Gently spoon into the prepared springform pan. Place the pan into a large roasting pan. Add water to the roasting pan until water reaches halfway up the side of springform pan.

Bake until the center is set, 1 to 1¼ hours. Let the cake stand in the water for 30 minutes. Remove to a wire rack and loosen the sides of the pan; cool completely. The cake can be served chilled or at room temperature.

The cake lasts up to 1 week well wrapped in the refrigerator.

Makes 16 to 20 servings.

Note

If you don't have almond butter, all-natural peanut butter also works well.

BAKING WITH CHOCOLATE

Chocolate plays an extraordinary role in baking. While other flavorings merely perfume cakes, cookies, and pastries, chocolate infuses them with its presence—which is why the chocolate you use and the ways in which you handle it are so critical to successful baking.

If chocolate is the primary ingredient in a recipe, you owe it to yourself to select the best-quality chocolate you can find. That may mean splurging a bit, but quality begets quality. Which is the best chocolate? The one that tastes best.

Chocolate chips are formulated to soften but retain their shape in cake batters during baking—even at temperatures far beyond the normal melting point of chocolate. They become solid again when cooled slowly in baked cakes, sometimes taking as long as eight hours to set. If you cut the cake too soon, the soft chips will smear and mar the appearance of the slice.

Many recipes call for melting chocolate chips. Rather than force chocolate chips to melt, substitute an equal amount of chocolate bars instead. Chocolate bars contain more cocoa butter than chocolate chips; as a result, they will melt more fluidly and blend into batters more easily.

The candy section of most supermarkets contains a variety of eating chocolates that are equally suitable for baking. Look for bars of chocolate that do not contain any inclusions, such as nuts, creams, raisins, and so on.

Melted chocolate should be slightly warm to tepid when you add it to a batter. If it's too warm, it may melt the butter or deflate the eggs. If it's too cold, it may solidify in the batter, causing it to appear speckled.

—*Elaine González*

COMFORTABLE BISTRO SUPPER

Smoked Trout Spread with Horseradish*

Frisée Green Salad

Roast Chickens with Shallots and Tarragon*

French Baguettes and Butter

Lemon Soufflé Crepes*

WINE RECOMMENDATIONS:

For first course: Champagne or Alsace Riesling

For main course: White: Loire or Napa Sauvignon Blanc or a crisp Pinot Gris

Red: Medium-bodied, dry-fruited Pinot Noir

SMOKED TROUT SPREAD WITH HORSERADISH

A quick standby for a dinner party for friends, I often vary the spread by adding freshly chopped herbs, such as chives, parsley, or tarragon.

— *Carol Mighton Haddix*

- 1 smoked trout, about 10 ounces, *or* 2 smoked trout fillets, about 8 ounces
- 1 cup sour cream, *or* crème fraîche
- 1 tablespoon prepared horseradish
- ½ teaspoon freshly ground black pepper
  Cocktail pumpernickel bread slices, cut in half into triangles
  Fresh dill for garnish (optional)

Skin the trout; flake meat into medium bowl, removing any large bones. Stir in sour cream, horseradish, and pepper. Spread over bread. Garnish with dill if desired.

Makes 8 appetizer servings (about 1¾ cups).

ROAST CHICKENS WITH SHALLOTS AND TARRAGON

Fresh shallots and tarragon add a burst of flavor to this simple roast chicken preparation. It is so easy to prepare (and appealing to all ages) that it has become my staple for entertaining throughout the seasons

— Abby Mandel

¼ cup olive oil

4 small chickens (about 2½ pounds each), preferably organic, fat trimmed, rinsed, blotted dry

¼ cup seasoned salt

2 tablespoons lemon pepper

4 large shallots, peeled, halved

1 large bunch tarragon

Fresh tarragon sprigs, for garnish

Place the rack in the bottom third of the oven. Preheat the oven to 425°F. Rub oil on the chickens, inside and out. Combine the seasoned salt and lemon pepper in a small dish. Sprinkle on the chickens, inside and out. This can be done up to 12 hours ahead of time and refrigerated. Before roasting, let stand at room temperature for 30 minutes.

Fill the main cavity of each chicken with shallots and tarragon, dividing evenly. Tuck the wings under; tie the legs together. Place the chickens, breast-side down, on a rack set in a large, shallow roasting pan. Roast until lightly browned, about 30 minutes. Remove from the oven. Insert a large kitchen fork into the main cavity and turn breast-side up. Continue to roast until darkly browned and a meat thermometer inserted between the thigh and leg registers 165°F, about 25 minutes more (depending on the size of the chicken).

To serve, remove the shallots and tarragon and discard. Cut the chickens in half, removing backbones. Transfer the chickens to a warm platter. Garnish the platter with fresh tarragon sprigs. Serve hot, warm, or at room temperature.

Makes 8 servings.

LEMON SOUFFLÉ CREPES

When I worked at Maxim's de Paris, which was located in the Astor Tower Hotel (the original offshoot of the famed Parisian restaurant that opened in Chicago in 1963), the pastry chef labored all day preparing the desserts for the display cart wheeled into the dining room each evening. He also prepped his station for the special desserts that needed completion during dinner service, such as the soufflés. Chef Bernard Cretier would call out, "Lemon soufflé crepe, s'il vous plait," and I would turn on the electric mixer for the egg whites while heating the cream base on the pastry kitchen's stove. Lemon juice and zest were added to the warming pastry cream, a bit of sugar was added to the mixing whites to stabilize them, and the two were stirred together and spooned inside a crepe folded in half for baking in the oven. As if by magic, the soufflé would expand and puff up, opening the crepe. A sprinkle of powdered sugar was the only garnish needed as waiters whisked this delicacy out into the dining room before it started to collapse. Preparing this soufflé dessert is one of the best memories of my time at Maxim's. Here is the recipe from the late Joanne Will's Chicago Tribune *article in 1976 with slight alterations — notably, less sugar in the crepe batter.*   —Jill Van Cleave

CREPES:

1	cup sifted all-purpose flour
2	tablespoons granulated sugar
⅛	teaspoon salt
2	large eggs
1	cup whole milk
¼	teaspoon pure vanilla extract
2	tablespoons unsalted butter, melted

SOUFFLÉ FILLING:

2½	tablespoons unsalted butter
2½	tablespoons all-purpose flour
1	cup granulated sugar, divided
⅛	teaspoon salt
⅔	cup whole milk
4	teaspoons grated lemon rind (colored part only)
¼	cup fresh lemon juice
4	egg yolks, slightly beaten
¼	teaspoon pure vanilla extract
8	egg whites, at room temperature
	Confectioners' sugar, sifted (optional)

For crepes, mix flour, sugar and salt in medium bowl. Whisk together eggs, milk and vanilla in a large bowl until well blended. Gradually whisk in dry ingredients, mixing just until blended. The batter should be smooth and just thick enough to coat whisk. If it is too thick, add a little more milk. Add the melted butter, whisking until blended. Let the batter rest for 30 minutes.

Preheat a 10-inch nonstick skillet or omelet pan over medium heat. Ladle a scant ¼ cup crepe batter into pan. Lift the pan slightly, turning it in a circular motion, to spread batter evenly on the bottom. (Crepe should be 8 inches in diameter.) Brown only lightly on the underside, about 30 seconds, then turn crepe over and cook the second side until golden, 15 to 20 seconds more. Slide the crepe onto a plate. Repeat this sequence, stacking crepes one on top of the other. (Crepes can be prepared ahead and refrigerated or even frozen for later use. If made ahead, separate stacked crepes with squares of waxed paper between each.)

For the soufflé filling, melt butter in a heavy-bottomed saucepan; blend in flour, ⅓ cup of the sugar, and salt. Slowly whisk in the milk until smooth. Cook over medium heat, stirring constantly, until the mixture boils and thickens. Remove the pan from heat. Whisk together the lemon rind, lemon juice, egg yolks and vanilla in a medium bowl until well blended. Whisk the mixture into hot sauce. Return the pan to heat and cook, while whisking, until the sauce thickens again, about 2 to 3 minutes. Do not boil. (Sauce may be made in advance and refrigerated. When ready to bake crepes, reheat sauce over medium-low heat, whisking until smooth.)

Preheat the oven to 450°F. Lightly butter two large baking dishes or baking sheets and set aside. In the large bowl of an electric mixer, beat the egg whites until soft peaks form. Gradually beat in the remaining ⅔ cup sugar until the whites are stiff, but not dry. Gently fold a large spoonful of the beaten whites into the hot sauce to lighten it. Add the hot mixture to the remaining beaten whites in the bowl; use a large rubber spatula to fold mixture gently until blended.

Spoon a very generous portion of soufflé filling in the center of each crepe, bringing the outside edges straight up and laying the crepe onto one side. Arrange them side-by-side in a baking dish. Bake until puffed and browned, 8 to 10 minutes. Sprinkle with confectioners' sugar and serve immediately.

Makes 8 servings.

GIVING A PARTY?

Remember, you are the hostess, so try to plan your meal so you can spend time with your guests rather than be stuck in the kitchen for the whole party.

- Try to add a "personal" touch that makes your table unique.

- Do not be afraid to mix china or favorite old silver pieces. It can add interest to your table.

- Remember to include extra glassware for the cocktail hour.

- If possible, set the table or gather platters, linen, serving pieces, and so on several days in advance, just in case you need extra items.

- Be prepared for an extra person or special dietary needs.

- Use candles to add a feeling of warmth and style to your table.

- If you plan to use flowers on the table, be sensitive to conversation as well as fragrance with food. Choose low arrangements and flowers with little scent.

- Most importantly, enjoy your guests.

—Linda Goodman

CELEBRATING SPRING

Chilled Spinach and Cucumber Soup*

Pasta with Fresh Herbs*

Crusty Dinner Rolls

Strawberry and Rhubarb Crisp*

WINE RECOMMENDATIONS:

White: Tokai Friulano or light Sauvignon Blanc

Red: Low-acid, nontannic Sangiovese or Grenache

CHILLED SPINACH AND CUCUMBER SOUP

Here is a recipe from the late Leslee Reis, shared by her friend, Nancy Brussat Barocci:

"A Grande Dame, Leslee entered a room with bravado and style. Everyone felt her energy. She was outspoken, direct, clear, and always hilarious. Her passion for food, wine, flowers, and art was clearly evident in her warm and charming Evanston restaurant Café Provencal, which received national acclaim. She was a huge presence, and an innovative and bold leader in the Chicago culinary scene. She is still missed to this day."

1	large onion, coarsely chopped
3	tablespoons olive oil
4	medium cucumbers, peeled, seeded, coarsely chopped
2	cloves garlic, minced
2	tablespoons chopped fresh dill
5	cups chicken broth, preferably homemade
10	ounces fresh leaf spinach, well-cleaned
2	teaspoons salt
½	teaspoon freshly ground white pepper
	Whipping cream, *or* crème fraîche (optional)

Cook the onion in the olive oil in a large saucepan over medium heat, stirring often, until transparent, about 10 minutes. Add the cucumbers, garlic, and half of the dill. Cook and stir another 10 minutes. Add the broth and simmer over medium-low heat until the cucumbers are tender but not mushy, about 15 minutes. Meanwhile, remove the spinach stems and tear any large leaves into smaller pieces. Add the spinach leaves to the cucumber mixture and simmer just until the spinach wilts, 1 to 2 minutes.

Add the remaining dill and season to taste with salt and white pepper. Serve as is, peasant-style, or purée until smooth for a more elegant presentation.

If desired, add a spoonful of cream or crème fraîche to each bowl just before serving. Soup can be served hot or cold.

Makes 8 servings (about 1 cup each).

PASTA WITH FRESH HERBS

This recipe comes from a friend of mine in the Liguria region of Italy. It features many of the fresh herbs grown and beloved in that region. She prepared it for me during a trip to Italy, and now I enjoy making it with my homegrown herbs. —*Maria Battaglia*

SAUCE:

4	pounds fresh ripe plum tomatoes, or 1 can (28 ounces) plum tomatoes
6	tablespoons extra virgin olive oil
2	tablespoons butter
1	teaspoon salt
½	teaspoon crushed red pepper flakes (optional)

PASTA:

½	cup pine nuts
½	cup fresh basil leaves
½	cup fresh Italian parsley leaves
¼	cup fresh oregano leaves
¼	cup fresh thyme leaves
¼	cup fresh rosemary leaves
2	fresh sage leaves (optional)
2	small cloves garlic
2	pounds fresh pasta or 1 pound dried pasta
2	cups grated Parmigiano-Reggiano cheese

For sauce, purée tomatoes in a food mill; place in a large saucepan. Add olive oil, butter, salt, and red pepper flakes. Simmer, uncovered, until sauce reduces and thickens slightly, about 20 minutes.

Bring 8 quarts of water to a boil for the pasta. Chop the pine nuts, herbs, and garlic; mix and set aside. When the water comes to a boil, add salt and return to a boil. Add pasta and cook 3 to 5 minutes (12 to 13 minutes for dry pasta) to al dente. Drain in a colander.

Place cooked pasta in a warm, shallow pasta bowl. Working quickly, add the herb mixture and toss well. Add the grated cheese and toss again. Keep tossing so the cheese melts over the hot pasta. Finally, add enough sauce to coat the pasta evenly. Toss well and serve immediately. This dish can also be served at room temperature, which makes it ideal for picnics and buffets.

Makes 8 servings.

STRAWBERRY AND RHUBARB CRISP

It is so easy to celebrate the taste of spring with this combination of fresh strawberries and rhubarb. The buttery brown sugar topping includes pecans, which add both flavor and texture to this luscious dessert. Be sure to make Chicago's Green City Market, or your local farmer's market, your first stop when shopping for this recipe.

—*Abby Mandel*

1½ pounds fresh rhubarb, cut into ½-inch thick slices, about 6 cups

2½ pints strawberries, rinsed, blotted dry, hulled, cut in half or quarters, if large

1¼ cups granulated sugar

3   tablespoons plus 1 teaspoon quick-cooking tapioca

2   tablespoons fresh orange juice

1   tablespoon finely grated orange rind (colored part only)

2   teaspoons pure vanilla extract

¼   teaspoon ground allspice

BROWN SUGAR CRISP TOPPING:

1   cup all-purpose flour

⅔   cup packed brown sugar

1   teaspoon ground cinnamon

⅛   teaspoon salt

½   cup (1 stick) unsalted butter, softened, cut into 4 pieces

¾   cup pecan halves

Vanilla ice cream, for serving

Preheat the oven to 350°F. Set aside a large, shallow baking dish or a 13 x 9-inch nonaluminum baking pan.

Put the rhubarb, strawberries, granulated sugar, tapioca, juice, orange rind, vanilla, and allspice in the baking pan. Use your hands to toss until well mixed. Let stand 20 to 30 minutes, stirring once midway through. Spread fruit evenly over baking pan.

For brown sugar crisp topping, put the flour, brown sugar, cinnamon and salt into food processor bowl fitted with metal blade. Process quickly to mix, about 2 seconds. Scatter the butter and pecans over flour. Pulse the processor until mixture is crumbly but not massing together, about 20 to 30 seconds.

Sprinkle the Brown Sugar Crisp Topping evenly over fruit. Place the dish on a large cookie sheet or on a large sheet of heavy-duty foil to catch any bubbling juices.

Bake until the top is browned and juices are bubbling, about 1 hour. Let cool at least 1 hour before serving. Serve warm with small scoops of ice cream.

Makes 8 to 10 servings.

Notes

Crisp can be refrigerated overnight with an airtight cover. Before serving, let the Crisp sit uncovered until it comes to room temperature. Reheat, uncovered, in 350°F oven until warm, about 12 minutes.

The Brown Sugar Crisp topping can be used immediately, stored up to 2 days in refrigerator, or frozen up to 1 month, wrapped airtight in double plastic bags to ensure freshness. It is not necessary to thaw the topping before using. If the topping compacts during freezing, work through the bag with your hands to crumble it

A JEWISH HOLIDAY FEAST

Chopped Chicken Liver*

Savory Holiday Brisket*

Potato Pancakes

Steamed Baby Carrots and Pearl Onions

Lemon Sponge Cake*

WINE RECOMMENDATIONS:

For first course: Medium dry Madeira or sherry

For main course: Full-bodied, red-fruited, low-tannin wines such as Cotes du Rhone, Australian Grenache / Syrah / Mourvedre, or Tuscany's Sangiovese

CHOPPED CHICKEN LIVER

This chopped liver was made for every holiday as long as I can remember. My mother loved making it, my grandmother loved making it, I love making it, and our customers at Fox & Obel love it. We all love it, because it is always a big hit. My grandmother chopped it in a bowl, and my mother used a meat grinder that she attached to the counter. Today, I use a food processor.

— *Meme Hopmayer*

3 tablespoons rendered chicken schmaltz (fat)
2 very large onions, thinly sliced (about 1½ pounds total)
1 pound chicken livers
2 hard-cooked eggs, peeled
3 cloves garlic, roasted
Salt and freshly ground pepper, to taste
Cornichons (optional)
Matzoh, crackers, *or* toasted French bread slices, for serving

Melt the schmaltz over medium heat in a large skillet. Add onions and cook over medium heat, stirring occasionally, until golden and caramelized, about 30 minutes. Pat the chicken livers dry with paper towels. Add to the cooked onions. Increase heat to medium-high and cook until the chicken livers' centers are slightly pink and juices have evaporated, 5 to 7 minutes. Add the roasted garlic, salt, and pepper. If mixture seems dry, add a little more schmaltz.

Allow the mixture to cool to room temperature. Place all the ingredients in a food processor and process until chopped, but not puréed. Season with salt and pepper. Place into 2-cup quart mold or container and refrigerate overnight. Unmold and garnish with cornichons. Serve at room temperature with matzoh, crackers, or French bread slices.

Makes about 12 appetizer servings (about 2¾ cups).

Note
To roast garlic, remove the excess papery skin from a whole head of garlic cloves. Cut about ¼ off the top of the head, exposing the cloves. Place the head on a small sheet of aluminum foil and drizzle with 1 teaspoon olive oil. Wrap the head in foil; place on a cooking sheet. Bake in 400°F oven or toaster oven until tender, 40 to 45 minutes.

SAVORY HOLIDAY BRISKET

My classic holiday brisket always receives raves when I am entertaining. This recipe can be prepared ahead of time and reheated—it actually tastes better this way! I like to cook a large brisket so I have plenty of leftovers.

—Carol Smoler

- 1   tablespoon vegetable oil
- 1   beef brisket (5 to 6 pounds)
- 1   large onion, thinly sliced
       Salt and freshly ground pepper, to taste
- 1   can (28 ounces) tomato sauce
- 1   envelope (0.95 ounces) Kosher, or reduced-sodium, onion soup mix
- 1   bottle (12 ounces) chili sauce (such as Bennett's brand)

Preheat the oven to 325°F. Heat oil in a large roasting pan or Dutch oven over medium heat until hot. Place the brisket and onion in the pan; cook, turning the brisket and stirring the onions, until evenly browned, about 10 minutes. Season with salt and pepper.

Combine the tomato sauce, onion soup mix, and chili sauce; pour over the brisket in the pan. Add water, if needed, so the brisket is submerged in liquid. Cover tightly; roast until brisket is fork-tender, 3½ to 4 hours.

Remove the brisket from the sauce. Refrigerate the brisket and sauce separately overnight.

To serve, remove and discard the fat from the cold sauce. Heat the sauce over medium heat in a large saucepan; simmer until slightly thickened. Slice the brisket (against the grain) on a diagonal into thin slices. Nestle into the warmed sauce. Serve hot.

Makes 12 to 16 servings.

Notes

Brisket is not always available, so call ahead and special-order your brisket a few days before the holiday.

LEMON SPONGE CAKE

This is our Passover sponge cake. My mother always made it for Passover, and even though we loved this cake, it was never made any other time. Sometimes, she made two cakes, and we used one to make a trifle. My mother loved to bake, and she also loved to wear artificial red nails. We used to joke that whoever got the piece of cake with an artificial nail in it got to take home the leftovers.　　　　　—*Meme Hopmayer*

7	large eggs, separated, at room temperature
1	whole egg, at room temperature
1½	cups granulated sugar, sifted
	Grated rind (colored part only) of 1 large lemon
⅓	cup fresh lemon juice
¾	cup sifted potato starch
½	teaspoon baking powder
	Dash of salt

Preheat the oven to 350°F. Beat 7 egg yolks and 1 whole egg in the large bowl of an electric mixer until frothy, thick, and lemon-colored, about 3 minutes. Gradually beat in sifted sugar, lemon rind, and juice, beating constantly. Combine the potato starch with baking powder and salt. Gradually add the starch mixture to the egg mixture by spoonfuls, beating until smooth.

Beat the egg whites in a clean, large electric mixer bowl until stiff but not dry. Using a rubber spatula, carefully fold the egg whites into the egg yolk mixture. Spoon into an ungreased 10-inch angel food cake pan. Bake until a wooden pick comes out dry, 45 to 50 minutes. Remove from the oven and place the pan upside down on rack to cool completely.

Loosen cake with a knife; remove the cake from the pan. Use a serrated knife to cut the cake into wedges for serving.

Makes 12 servings.

COME FOR BRUNCH

Sparkling Berry Cocktail*

Cantaloupe Slices with Blueberries

Savory Egg Pie*

Banana Bread*

Fresh-Squeezed Orange Juice, Coffee, and Tea

WINE RECOMMENDATIONS:

Sparkling wines or a mineral-noted off-dry Riesling

SPARKLING BERRY COCKTAIL

This colorful cocktail recipe, given to me by a friend in Door County, offers a fun start to any brunch.

— *Camilla Nielsen*

1   cup Berry Purée (recipe follows)
1   cup Cointreau, *or* other orange-flavored, liqueur
1   bottle (750 ml) dry sparkling wine, chilled

For each cocktail, spoon 2 tablespoons of Berry Purée into a fluted glass. Add 2 tablespoons of orange liqueur; stir to mix. Top with sparkling wine.

Makes 8 servings.

BERRY PURÉE

1   pint fresh strawberries, hulled
½   pint fresh raspberries
1   vanilla bean, split
1   teaspoon sugar
2   tablespoons fresh lime juice

Combine the strawberries and raspberries in a food processor or blender. Pulse to finely chop berries, then process to purée. Transfer the purée to small, heavy-bottomed saucepan; add the vanilla bean and sugar. Cook over low heat, stirring often, until the mixture is reduced to 1½ cups, about 45 minutes. Remove the vanilla bean; strain the thickened purée through a fine sieve into a small bowl. Discard the seedy pulp that remains in the sieve. Cool the strained purée. Stir in lime juice. Store in a covered container in the refrigerator.

Makes about 1 cup.

SAVORY EGG PIE

This is a favorite breakfast entrée from The Cake Stand Inn (my bed & breakfast in Pecos, New Mexico). It is perfect for brunch when accompanied by a wonderful salad or fruit. The leftovers are excellent, too!

—Linda Goodman

8   ounces thickly sliced bacon

4   ounces fresh mushrooms, quartered

1   red, yellow, *or* orange bell pepper, seeded, chopped

3   ounces soft goat cheese, crumbled

½   cup freshly grated Parmesan cheese

2   tablespoons chopped fresh thyme

5   large eggs

1½ cups heavy (whipping) cream

½   teaspoon salt

½   teaspoon freshly ground black pepper

Preheat the oven to 325°F. Generously butter a 10-inch glass pie plate. Cook the bacon in a large skillet until crisp. Remove; drain on paper towels. Pour off all but 2 tablespoons of the bacon fat from the skillet. Return the skillet to heat. Add the mushrooms and cook over high heat until browned, about 5 minutes. Spread the mushrooms in the prepared pie plate. Crumble the bacon over the mushrooms. Sprinkle with red bell pepper, cheeses, and thyme.

Beat the eggs and cream in a large bowl; season with salt and pepper. Gently pour the egg mixture over the vegetable mixture. Bake until the eggs are set in the center and the top is golden brown, about 1 hour. Cool on a wire rack about 10 minutes before serving.

Makes 8 servings.

A QUICK CAVIAR PRIMER

When you are entertaining, using caviar is a quick and easy way to present glorious food. It is also an easy way to flavor dishes from course to course. According to the strictest traditional rules, caviar is the roe (eggs) of a female sturgeon from the Caspian Sea. Today, any cured roe is considered to be caviar as long as it is preceded by the fish species' name.

It all started in the 1920s, when the Iranian-born, Russian-raised Petrossian brothers introduced caviar to Parisian society. Today, the U.S. imports the most of this traditional delicacy, and it is largely forgotten that throughout the 1800s, the U.S. produced 80 percent of the world's best sturgeon caviar. The legendary Lake Sturgeon was overfished, and its spawning waters were destroyed or made inaccessible. In 1910, the U.S. caviar industry shut down—just as the Russian one began.

Sadly, history is close to repeating itself. In 2006, the U.S. Department of Fish & Wildlife placed a total ban on imports of caviar from the most sought-after Caspian Sea sturgeon, the beluga. It is hoped that stopping the harvest will allow the beluga to reestablish itself before it disappears. Caspian sevruga and oesetra caviar seems safe for now, and many new fish farms are dedicated to raising beluga.

This is an important time for "other" caviars to be introduced, used, and appreciated. There are many kinds of sturgeon available—both farmed and wild. Hackleback and paddlefish are extremely common in U.S. waters, and they make beautiful black roe that in the past was often unscrupulously sold as "imported." American waters also produce whitefish, salmon, trout, and bowfin caviars that lend themselves to use in recipes. The Japanese have introduced tobikko (tuna roe), which offers several versatile flavors and colors.

When buying caviar, know your vendor. He or she should be able to tell you how long it will stay fresh, if it can be frozen, or if it has been vacuum packed, pasteurized, or has any added shelf-life extenders. In general, the watery eggs from whitefish, salmon and tobikko are easily stored and sold frozen, whereas the fatty ones from sturgeon and paddlefish can be frozen only within days of processing. Most companies do not do so.

Caviar is versatile. Try adding it to eggs for a brunch party. For soft-boiled eggs, take off the tops and with a toothpick or demitasse spoon, stir hackleback sturgeon caviar into the soft yolk. Top an omelet with a dollop of sour cream laced with minced chives and a sprinkle of salmon roe caviar for the finale. Try floating whipped cream on soup topped with caviar. For salads, stir the eggs into the dressing. Add bowfin caviar to the traditional horseradish sauce for roast beef. Any fish sautéed in a flavored butter sauce can have a last-minute dollop of caviar added.

—Carolyn Collins

BANANA BREAD

This recipe was passed down to me from my grandmother, Frances Redman. My mother used to bake this banana bread recipe every year in empty soup cans, and we would give them to teachers and neighbors as Christmas gifts.

—Michaele Musel

1	cup granulated sugar
½	cup (1 stick) unsalted butter, softened
2	large eggs, beaten
3	tablespoons sour milk (see note)
3	large very ripe bananas, coarsely mashed
2	cups all-purpose flour
1	teaspoon baking soda
1	teaspoon baking powder
¾	teaspoon salt

Preheat the oven to 375°F. Grease a 9- by 5-inch loaf pan. In a large bowl, mix together the ingredients in the order they are listed until just combined. Spoon the batter into the prepared pan. Bake until wooden pick inserted in center comes out clean, 50 to 60 minutes. Cool on wire rack about 10 minutes. Unmold from pan and cool completely on rack.

Makes 8 to 12 servings.

Note

To make sour milk, add 1 tablespoon cider vinegar to 3 tablespoons whole milk.

FROM THE GRILL

Roasted Pepper Salad with Basil and Goat Cheese*

Rosemary Marinated Grilled Lamb*

Couscous or Rice Pilaf

Organic Blueberry Bread Pudding*

WINE RECOMMENDATIONS:

Dry red with earthy, herbal notes,
such as northern Rhone Syrah or left-bank Bordeaux

ROASTED PEPPER SALAD WITH BASIL AND GOAT CHEESE

I developed this recipe and brought it to several Les Dames functions, where it quickly became a favorite of two early members of our Chicago chapter, Katherine Smith and Marian Tripp. The salad is best made with the lovely goat cheese named for another member, Sofia Solomon: Capriole Farm's award-winning "Sofia."

—Karen Levin

3	medium red bell peppers
3	medium yellow bell peppers
⅓	cup extra virgin olive oil
3	tablespoons balsamic vinegar
2	teaspoons Dijon-style, or hot Dijon-style, mustard
1	teaspoon minced garlic
½	teaspoon salt
½	teaspoon sugar
¼	teaspoon freshly ground black pepper
¼	cup thinly sliced basil leaves
4	ounces best quality goat cheese, crumbled

Preheat the broiler. Cut the peppers lengthwise into quarters; discard stems and seeds. Place the peppers skin-side-up on a foil-lined jelly roll pan or baking sheet. Broil 3 to 4 inches from the heat source until the skin is evenly blackened, 12 to 14 minutes. Wrap the peppers up in the foil from the pan and let stand at room temperature 10 minutes.

Meanwhile, combine oil, vinegar, mustard, garlic, salt, sugar, and pepper in a small bowl and whisk together to combine into the dressing. Unwrap peppers. Working over the foil, peel off and discard blackened skin. Pour any accumulated pepper juices from the foil into the dressing.

Arrange the peppers attractively in a shallow 1½ quart oval or round serving dish. Whisk the dressing and drizzle over peppers. Let stand at room temperature 30 minutes, or cover and refrigerate up to 2 days. Before serving, bring to room temperature and top with the basil and goat cheese. Top with additional freshly ground black pepper if desired.

Makes 8 servings.

ENJOYING CHEESE, WINE, AND BREAD

Perhaps the earliest culinary gifts to mankind were the fruit of the vine, milk curdled into cheese, and grains baked into loaves of all shapes, flavors, and sizes. This natural trio is basic to Western gastronomy, and for centuries it has provided pleasure and sustenance to shepherds in the field, harvesters in the vineyard, and pilgrims through their travels. Fast-forward to today, and the pairing of wine, cheese, and bread features in many scenarios: wine tastings, picnics, snacks, multicourse banquets, appetizers, and complete meals. In terms of enjoyment, wine and cheese accompanied with savory bread offer pleasure beyond measure.

We customarily serve white wines before red, and light-bodied before full-bodied wines. However, the danger of this practice is that as a menu progresses, this often sets the biggest, boldest red with the cheese course, where a wine's power can overwhelm, the red berry flavors often clash, and the tannins bring out bitterness. A recent University of California Davis study showed that flavorful cheese dulls the taste of red wine, making it difficult to discern specific flavors.

Therefore, the caution flags are up, and with a cheese pairing, it is wise to choose red wines with softer tannins, such as Pinot Noir, Loire Cabernet Franc, Gamay, and Garnacha. You may also serve wines vinified for early drinking, or mature wines that have mellowed. Semi-hard, particularly aged cheeses, such as Gruyere, Emmenthal, Cheddar and sheep's milk cheeses, call for these specific varieties of red wine.

On the other hand, white wines with tree-fruit flavors (apple, pear, and citrus), seductive aromatics, clean minerality, crisp acidity, a lack of tannins, and marvelous textural interest are compatible with a broad range of cheeses. Champagne and other brut sparkling wines cleanse the palate of fat and salt and are particularly suited to soft-ripened cheeses. Goat cheeses with crisp, dry Sauvignon Blanc, Munster paired with a heady Gewurztraminer, and Epoisses with a rich, aromatic Pinot Gris are all classic matches. A cool-climate, well-bred Riesling is always appropriate.

Sweet dessert wines—Sauternes and Vin Doux Natural, for example—and the fortified wines, such as Port, Madeira, and Sherry, are traditional partners to sharp, salty, blue-veined cheeses, such as Stilton, Roquefort, and Gorgonzola.

At tastings and large parties, several cheeses are usually offered on appropriate cheese serving plates or cheese boards, with the selection including cow's-, goat's-, and sheep's-milk cheeses. A variation in color, shape, and flavor also adds appeal. In France, the cheese cart frequently carries 15 or more different cheeses, with each one being site-, season-, and age-specific. Whether your taste runs to white or red wine for a more complex offering, it's wise to recognize that the cheese will mask many of the subtleties of a fine wine. This is where bread—earthy, whole-grained, flat or course-textured, or bursting with nuts or raisins—plays an important role. The texture adds appeal and enhances each delectable taste.

There is no magic key to open the pleasures of wine, cheese, and bread—just an appreciation of the complexities of each and the simplicity of their traditional appeal.

—*Barbara Glunz-Donovan*

ROSEMARY-MARINATED GRILLED LAMB

This grilled butterflied leg of lamb is a classic Chez Madelaine recipe. I serve it at Easter and teach it to evening couples groups in the summer and fall.

—*Madelaine Bullwinkel*

1	boneless, butterflied leg of lamb (about 4 pounds)
	Coarse (kosher) salt and freshly ground black pepper, to taste
1	tablespoon fresh rosemary leaves, snipped into ¼-inch pieces
4	large cloves garlic, peeled and thinly sliced
	Olive oil

Lightly sprinkle both sides of the meat with salt, pepper, rosemary and thin slivers of garlic. Seal in plastic wrap and refrigerate overnight.

Remove the lamb from refrigerator 1 hour prior to cooking. Place several skewers through the pieces of lamb diagonally to secure it into a single roast. Build a charcoal fire or preheat a gas grill to medium heat.

Pat the lamb dry with paper towels, then lightly coat it with olive oil. Place lamb on grill rack directly over coals. Sear the meat for 10 minutes, uncovered, turning once. Close grill vents to half-open position. Cover the grill and continue roasting to medium-rare (145°F in its thickest portion), about 45 minutes.

Let the meat stand 15 minutes before carving into thin slices. If desired, sprinkle with a little coarse salt before serving.

Makes 8 servings.

Note

Oven roasting: Marinate and prepare the lamb for roasting as directed above, except do not skewer meat. Fold the butterflied leg into a solid piece and tie with butcher's string to secure. Preheat the oven to 450°F. Place the meat on a rack in a shallow roasting pan. Roast at 450°F 10 minutes. Reduce the oven temperature to 350°F and continue roasting to medium-rare (145°F in its thickest portion), about 45 minutes.

ORGANIC BLUEBERRY BREAD PUDDING

When I look at those gorgeous, delicious Michigan blueberries at the Green City Market every year, I want to create a whole menu around blueberries. I feel the same way about tomatoes in August!

I have clients who make sure they have blueberry bread pudding at their events every summer. I always prefer to use organic eggs, milk, cream, and blueberries. This recipe is a reason to have a party!

—*Rita Gutekanst*

4	large eggs
⅔	cup packed light brown sugar
2	cups whole milk
2	cups heavy (whipping) cream
2	tablespoons pure vanilla extract, *or* vanilla bean paste
¼	teaspoon freshly ground mace
¼	teaspoon freshly ground nutmeg
¼	teaspoon ground cinnamon
18	slices day-old French baguette
½	cup (1 stick) butter, melted
2	cups fresh blueberries
	Vanilla bean ice cream (optional)

Preheat the oven to 350°F. Combine the eggs, brown sugar, milk, cream, vanilla, mace, nutmeg, and cinnamon in a large bowl. Mix well to dissolve the sugar. Brush the bread pieces with melted butter on both sides. Place the bread in a buttered 13 x 9-inch pan. Sprinkle evenly with the blueberries. Pour the egg mixture over the bread.

Let stand 15 minutes to allow the bread to soak. Bake until the center is set, but slightly jiggly, 40 to 50 minutes. Let cool on a wire rack to room temperature. Cool completely in the refrigerator until firm.

Serve with vanilla bean ice cream. For a special touch, cut into serving pieces using a 3-inch round cutter.

Makes 8 servings.

FISHERMAN'S FEAST

Hickory Smoked Bacon Wrapped Rainbow Trout*

Cheddar Cheese Grits*

Sautéed Greens with a Kick*

Ice Cream Sundaes

WINE RECOMMENDATIONS:

White: Moderately-oaked Chardonnay, off-dry Chenin or Provençal dry Rosé

Red: Light-bodied Merlot

HICKORY SMOKED BACON WRAPPED RAINBOW TROUT

This whole trout is impressive to serve and easy to prepare. Season it simply with olive oil and salt before stuffing it with fresh tarragon and wrapping it in thick hickory-smoked bacon. The bacon adds flavor, bastes the trout while it grills, and prevents any sticking. Keeping the head and tail on the fish while it grills results in better flavor and helps keep the fish intact during the cooking time. This recipe is adapted from Taming the Flame: Secrets for Hot-and-Quick Grilling and Low-and-Slow BBQ *(John Wiley & Sons).*

—*Elizabeth Karmel*

4 whole trout (about 1 pound per fish), cleaned, with head and tail on
  Olive oil
  Coarse (kosher) salt
1 to 2 bunches fresh tarragon, or favorite fresh herb
12 slices hickory smoked bacon, at room temperature

Pat the trout dry with paper towels. Brush the trout inside and out with olive oil and season with salt. Stuff each fish cavity with ¼ of the tarragon. Do not cut or remove stems. Close fish and, starting at the head just beneath the eye, begin to wrap the bacon around the fish, slightly overlapping, until the fish is completely covered (each fish will need about 3 pieces of bacon). Stop wrapping when you get to the last inch of the tail. Place wrapped fish on a clean platter. (This step can be done up to 1 day in advance. If doing in advance, cover the fish tightly and refrigerate until ready to grill.)

Build a charcoal fire and arrange the coals for indirect cooking or preheat a gas grill to medium-high. Place fish in center of cooking grate over indirect heat and grill for 10 minutes. Turn the fish; continue to cook until the fish flakes and is cooked through, 5 to 10 minutes more. Remove from the grill and serve immediately.

Makes 4 servings.

Variation
Preheat the oven to 375°F. Place the bacon-wrapped trout on a rack fitted into a baking sheet with sides. Roast in the oven until fish flakes and is cooked through, 16 to 20 minutes.

CHEDDAR CHEESE GRITS

I love grits. Although I didn't grow up in the South, I did grow up with Southern friends and learned to appreciate this regional favorite. When I discovered that I could enjoy grits at meals other than breakfast, I was elated and encouraged. I served this recipe at my daughter's wedding. —*Nancy Harris*

3½ to 4 cups water
1½ teaspoons salt
1 cup white grits, stone-ground preferred
¼ cup heavy (whipping) cream
8 ounces Cheddar cheese, shredded (about 1 cup)

Heat water and salt to a boil in a 2-quart saucepan. Slowly add the grits to the water while stirring. Reduce heat; simmer covered, stirring frequently, for 30 minutes. If the grits become too thick, thin with a little water. Just before serving, add the cream and cheese and stir until the cheese is melted.

Makes 4 generous servings.

SAUTÉED GREENS WITH A KICK

Many people like to cook greens until they are soft and completely tender, but I prefer them more crisp-tender and bright green. This method can be used for any greens, but kale might take more time to reach that crisp-tender stage. I often like to include the stems, too, and add them to the pan first to give them a head start.

—Carol Mighton Haddix

1   pound kale, or Swiss chard
2   tablespoons olive oil
2   shallots, finely chopped
2   cloves garlic, finely chopped
¼   teaspoon crushed red pepper flakes
¼   teaspoon salt

If using kale, remove and discard the stems; coarsely chop the leaves. If using Swiss chard, coarsely chop the stems and leaves, but keep them separate.

Heat the olive oil in a large skillet over medium heat. Add the shallots; cook, stirring, until softened and lightly golden, 3 minutes. Add the garlic; cook, stirring, 1 minute.

Add the kale greens (or chard stems) to the skillet; stir to coat with oil. Cover the skillet and cook until slightly softened, about 5 minutes. If using chard, add the leaves to the pan now. Uncover the skillet; continue to cook, until just tender, about 10 minutes longer. Stir in red pepper and salt.

Makes 4 generous servings.

ROOFTOP FIREWORKS PARTY

Fresh Garden Vegetables with Dill Dip

Grilled Pork Tenderloin with Peach Salsa and Spinach Salad*

Assorted Flatbreads and Crackers

Mile-High Fresh Blueberry Pie*

WINE RECOMMENDATIONS:

White: Dry, fruit-forward Semillon, Vouvray (Chenin Blanc) or German Riesling

Red: Bourgogne Rouge or other medium-bodied Pinot Noir

GRILLED PORK TENDERLOIN WITH PEACH SALSA AND SPINACH SALAD

This recipe is one of my favorites for summer beach vacations and spontaneous entertaining. It is easy to prepare and flavorful, and the colors of the dish are gorgeous, whether presented on plates or on communal platters. The pork tenderloin is rubbed with a zesty spice rub and topped with sweet, savory salsa, and the fresh spinach salad is tossed in a slightly sweet and spicy balsamic vinaigrette. Enjoy this recipe anytime you want a taste of summer!

—*Dana Benigno*

PORK TENDERLOIN:

- 2 teaspoons ground cumin
- 2 teaspoons paprika
- 2 teaspoons garlic powder
- 1 teaspoon dried oregano
- ½ teaspoon salt
  Dash of ground red pepper (cayenne)
  Olive oil (enough to make a paste from the spices)
- 2 pork tenderloins (about 12 to 16 ounces each)

PEACH SALSA:

- 3 large ripe peaches, peeled and chopped
- 2 tablespoons chopped fresh cilantro
- 3 tablespoons minced red onion
  Juice of ½ lime
- 1 tablespoon minced jalapeño, or other chili pepper (optional)
  Dash salt

SPINACH SALAD:

- ¼ cup balsamic vinegar
- 1 tablespoon pure maple syrup
- 1 teaspoon Dijon-style mustard
  Salt and freshly ground pepper, to taste
- ½ cup olive oil
- 1 medium red bell pepper, cored, sliced
- 4 ounces blue cheese, crumbled
- 4 ounces fresh mushrooms, sliced
- 2 tablespoons green onions, sliced
- 4 to 6 cups (9 ounces) baby spinach, stems removed, well rinsed, patted dry

For the pork, combine all spices in a small bowl. Stir in enough oil to make a paste. Rub the pork on all sides with the spice paste.

For peach salsa, combine the peaches, onion, cilantro, lime juice, jalapeño pepper, and salt in a medium bowl; toss to combine.

For spinach salad, combine the vinegar, syrup, mustard, salt, and pepper in the bottom of a large salad bowl; whisk together to combine. Add the olive oil; whisk together and set aside. Have the remaining salad ingredients ready.

Build a charcoal fire or preheat a gas grill to medium-high heat. Place the pork on the grill rack; cover and grill, turning occasionally, until the pork is slightly pink in the center, about 12 to 15 minutes. Transfer the pork to a wooden board, tent with foil, and let stand 10 minutes.

To serve, place all vegetables on top of the salad dressing and toss to coat. Carve the pork into thin slices. Serve the pork accompanied by the peach salsa and spinach salad.

Makes 4 servings.

MILE-HIGH FRESH BLUEBERRY PIE

The key to this summertime favorite is tossing the fresh berries with the hot sauce; the berries stay fresh-tasting and have a great texture. All that is needed is a garnish of fresh mint. — *Carol Smoler*

10 ounces frozen raspberries, thawed
⅔ cup granulated sugar
2 tablespoons cornstarch
¼ cup fresh lemon juice
3 pints fresh blueberries
1 9-inch pie crust shell, fully baked
　 Fresh mint leaves for garnish

Push the raspberries through a medium mesh strainer into a medium-size saucepan. Discard the seeds. Stir in the sugar. Heat the mixture to a boil; reduce heat to low. Dissolve the cornstarch in lemon juice in a small bowl; stir into the raspberry mixture. Cook and stir until the mixture clears and thickens. Remove the pan from heat. Gently fold in the blueberries to coat them with the sauce. Immediately pour them into the baked pie shell. Allow to cool to room temperature. Garnish with fresh mint leaves, if desired.

Makes 8 servings.

MEXICAN FIESTA

Summertime Margaritas*

Classic Guacamole*

Tortilla Chips and Salsa

Mexican Meatballs in Chipotle Chili Sauce*

Warm Tortillas

Crisp Green Salad

Mango Sorbet

WINE RECOMMENDATIONS:

Young, fruity California Zinfandel or nontannic Grenache/Garnacha

SUMMERTIME MARGARITAS

This is my favorite beverage to serve on the porch in the summertime. It's also the standard starter for Les Dames members and their guests who have attended the annual "Dames Who Drink" Ravinia Picnic for the past 10 years. The recipe doubles well if you are serving a crowd.
— Karen Levin

8   thin lime wedges
Coarse (kosher) salt
1½ cups premium, *or* gold, tequila
1⅓ cups frozen limeade concentrate (such as Minute Maid brand), not thawed
⅔   cup triple sec, Cointreau, *or* Grand Marnier liqueur
6   tablespoons fresh lime juice

Rub the rims of 8 glasses with one of the lime wedges. Place a layer of salt on a small plate. Dip the lime-coated glasses in the salt to lightly coat the rims.

Combine the remaining ingredients in a large pitcher, mixing until the concentrate thaws. Serve over ice in salt-rimmed glasses, or shake with ice cubes and strain into glasses. Garnish each margarita with a lime wedge.

Makes 8 servings.

PLANNING THE CHEESE COURSE

When you are presenting a cheese course, always offer a selection of milk varieties. For instance, if you are serving only three cheeses, offer one cow's milk, one goat's milk, and one sheep's milk variety.

Vary the rinds and textures. Offer a selection of natural, flourished, washed, waxy, oiled, or herbed rinds. Be certain to vary the textures, so not all of the cheeses are the same. Choose among creamy, semi-soft, firm, and hard types of cheese. For example, if you are offering a creamy flourished-rind cheese, such as Brillat-Savarin, also choose a firm option, such as Sainte-Maure, and a harder cheese, such as Petit Basque.

Vary the shapes and colors, if at all possible. If you are using a white blooming cheese, such as Camembert, also offer a rectangular brownish-rind cheese, such as Pont l'Eveque, or an orange-colored round cheese, such as Livarot, along with an ash-covered log, such as the Sainte-Maure, and a blue-veined cheese, such as Roquefort.

Choose seasonal or regional varieties of cheese. It is wonderful to be able to savor and celebrate a cheese that is only available at certain time of the year. For example, Vacherin Mont d'Or is available from November to January; Brousse from the Aveyron is only available for two weeks in March; and Provençal goat's milk cheeses

CLASSIC GUACAMOLE

I enjoy the flavor and predictable heat of serrano peppers in this classic guacamole—a favorite of our customers at Don Juan Restaurante on the northwest side of Chicago. Be sure to use avocados that are soft to the touch, but not too soft; otherwise, the guacamole will turn dark very quickly.   —*Maria Concannon*

4	ripe large avocados
¼	cup finely chopped onion
¼	cup fresh finely chopped cilantro
1	serrano chili pepper, seeded and finely chopped
	Salt, to taste
	Warm tortilla chips, for serving

Cut the avocados in half; remove the pits. Scoop the flesh into a large bowl. Coarsely chop with a fork. Stir in the onion, cilantro, and chili pepper. Add salt to taste. Serve with tortilla chips.

Makes 8 servings (about 3½ cups).

---

are a wonderful choice in the summertime, when the animals graze on the region's fresh pastures.

Cheeses contain living organisms and are constantly maturing. Proper care for cheeses requires a specific atmosphere with constant temperature; a good, but low, flow of air; and high humidity, to prevent them from drying out. A wine cellar is perfect. Standard refrigerators tend to be too cold and dry, and usually have poor air circulation. If there is no storage option to refrigeration, place the cheeses individually wrapped in wax paper (use aluminum foil for the blue cheeses) inside a hard plastic storage box for a short period of time. Open the box lid occasionally, or keep the lid slightly askew to allow aeration and to let gases escape from the cheeses. Usually, larger pieces of cheese keep longer than smaller portions. Ideally, purchase only enough cheese to last one week.

Always bring cheeses to room temperature before serving. Allow 1 to 2 hours, leaving small pieces wrapped and large pieces unwrapped. Remove paper from small cheeses ½ hour prior to serving. Cut the cheese a short time before serving, or risk drying it out.

Have fun! Experiment, and satisfy your own tastes. Remember the culinary trinity, the "three ferments": cheese, wine, and bread. Simplicity is often the best.

—*Sofia Solomon*

MEXICAN MEATBALLS IN CHIPOTLE CHILI SAUCE

Serve this recipe to guests who enjoy and appreciate the foods of Mexico. Using Mexican oregano and cinnamon adds to the authenticity of the dish. Make this combination a day ahead to enhance the flavors.

—*Marilyn Wilkinson*

MEATBALLS:

- 1 pound ground beef chuck
- 1 pound ground pork
- ½ cup minced flat leaf parsley
- 1 large white onion, grated
- 3 cloves garlic, minced
- 1 teaspoon dried Mexican oregano, *or* to taste
- ½ teaspoon ground cumin, *or* to taste
- 3 eggs, beaten
- 3 slices coarse white bread, crust removed and soaked in ⅓ cup milk
  Salt and freshly ground pepper, to taste

SAUCE:

- 6 large ripe tomatoes, or 1 can (28 ounces) fire-roasted whole tomatoes, drained
- 4 cloves garlic, peeled
- 1 medium onion, peeled, quartered
- 2½ cups chicken broth
- 1 to 3 canned chipotle chilies in adobo (to taste)
- 2 to 3-inch piece Mexican cinnamon bark, *or* 1 teaspoon ground cinnamon
- 2 teaspoons coarse (kosher) salt, *or* to taste
- 1 teaspoon freshly ground black pepper, *or* to taste
- ½ cup olive, *or* vegetable, oil
- 1 sprig mint, *or* pinch ground dried mint

For the meatballs, combine the meatball ingredients in a large bowl; mix with your hands. Refrigerate, covered, for 1 hour.

Meanwhile, for the sauce, if using fresh tomatoes, place on a cooking sheet and broil, turning once or twice until the skins blister and blacken, about 10 minutes. Peel the skin off tomatoes and place the peeled (or canned tomatoes) into a blender or food processor. Put the garlic and onion into a hot, dry skillet and cook, turning occasionally, over medium heat, until the garlic is lightly browned and the onion is lightly scorched. Add to the blender along with ½ cup of the broth, chipotles to taste (start with 1), cinnamon, salt and pepper. Blend until smooth. Taste, and add more chipotles if desired.

Heat oil in a large, heavy, and deep skillet over medium heat until quite hot but not smoking. Add the tomato mixture and "fry" until it thickens (it will splatter), about 10 minutes. Stir in the remaining 2 cups broth and heat to a boil. Stir in mint. Taste again, adjust salt and pepper, and add some adobo from the canned chilies if not spicy enough.

Shape the meat mixture into meatballs (about 1 inch diameter); the mixture should make 60 meatballs. Add the meatballs to the sauce. Shake the pan once or twice in the first five minutes of cooking to prevent sticking. Simmer slowly until the meatballs are done, about 30 minutes.

Makes 8 servings.

RISOTTO DINNER PARTY

Gourmet Food Shop Spread*

Turning Colors Salad*

Autumn Risotto*

Red Wine Poached Pears*

WINE RECOMMENDATIONS:

White: Sicilian white (Ansonica) or Campania's Fiano

Red: Piedmont's Nebbiolo

GOURMET FOOD SHOP SPREAD

There are so many wonderful products available in markets today. All one needs to do is peruse the shelves and deli cases of your local gourmet market or grocery store. Select a variety of dips or spreads, crackers, meats, and cheeses, and arrange them in bowls or plates on the kitchen counter close to where the cook will be preparing the risotto. —*Nancy Brussat Barocci*

SOME IDEAS AND RECOMMENDATIONS:

Green Olive Tapenade with Focaccia, Crackers, *or* Flatbread

Slices of a hard cheese, such as Manchego, Raschera, *or* Montasio

Slices of salami, such as Milano *or* Toscano

Bottled marinated mushrooms, artichokes, onions, *or* roasted red peppers

Marcona almonds, dried figs, and dates

Crispy bread sticks

TURNING COLORS SALAD

I always have a stack of recipes that I've clipped or that have been given to me. My house rule demands that a recipe cannot be filed without being tested, so only "keepers" are in the file. I like to try out new recipes on friends and ask them to give a "thumbs-up" or "thumbs-down." Only enthusiastic "thumbs-up" recipes are keepers. Here's a keeper. —*Katherine Smith*

8 cups mixed salad greens (such as mesclun mix)

1 can (14 ounces) water-packed quartered artichoke hearts, well drained

½ cup dried apricots, coarsely chopped

3 ounces thinly sliced prosciutto, cut into pieces (optional)

½ cup large walnut pieces, toasted (if desired)

¼ cup freshly grated Parmesan cheese

⅓ cup prepared red-wine vinaigrette, *or* Asian sesame ginger salad dressing

Combine all ingredients and toss with dressing; serve cold.

Makes 6 servings.

AUTUMN RISOTTO

I love the versatility of risotto: It can be simple or complex, depending on the ingredients added to the basic recipe. Risotto is the star and the main course in this menu. However, I often serve risotto as a first course and follow it with a dish that requires little time and preparation, such as veal scaloppini or a simple sautéed chop.

The best-known and most popular variety of Italian rice used for risotto is arborio rice. Arborio's uniform pearly kernels hold their shape, and their high starch content creates a delectable creamy consistency. Some chefs say the creamiest risotto is achieved when using another Italian rice variety, carnaroli. The starch content of this grain is even higher, and the end result is a luscious, plump risotto.

Because of its last-minute preparation, risotto can be a difficult dish to serve. However, making a good risotto requires more attention then concentration. My solution is to prepare this dish for good friends who will enjoy sharing a glass of wine and some simple hors d'oeuvres with the cook while she tends to the ceremonial stirring of the risotto.

—Nancy Brussat Barocci

2	tablespoons butter		1	tablespoon tomato paste
2	tablespoons olive oil		1	cup warm water
3	tablespoons finely chopped carrot		5	cups beef broth
3	tablespoons finely chopped celery		1½	cups arborio, *or* carnaroli, rice
2	tablespoons finely chopped onion		½	cup freshly grated Parmesan cheese
4	ounces lean ground beef			Salt, to taste
3	cups finely chopped cabbage			

Melt the butter with olive oil in a large, heavy-bottomed skillet over low heat. Add the carrot, celery, and onion; cook until soft. Add the ground beef and cook until no longer pink. Add the cabbage and the tomato paste, dissolved in the warm water. Cook gently until the mixture thickens and the water has evaporated, about 20 minutes. (This can be completed before the guests arrive, if desired.)

Bring the broth to a steady simmer in a large saucepan. Add the rice to the vegetable mixture and stir until it is thoroughly incorporated into the vegetable mixture. Cook for 2 minutes. Add ½ cup of simmering broth to the vegetable-rice mixture. After the rice has absorbed the broth, continue adding the broth, ½ cup at a time. Continue stirring over medium heat, making certain the rice is not sticking to the bottom of the pan and being careful not to add too much broth at one time. The rice is finished when it is firm but tender. This process will take approximately 20 to 25 minutes. If you run out of broth, use water.

When you estimate that the dish is a few minutes away from being done, add the Parmesan cheese and mix well. Add salt. Serve immediately.

Makes 4 to 6 servings.

RED WINE POACHED PEARS

An elegant finale to any meal, these poached pears can be prepared ahead and then filled with the mascarpone and garnished with the pecans and sauce at serving time. —*Nancy Brussat Barocci*

6	Bosc pears with stems
2	cups full-bodied red wine
2	tablespoons lemon juice
	Grated rind (colored part only) of 1 lemon
1	cup granulated sugar
1	stick cinnamon
1	vanilla bean, split
1	cup mascarpone cheese
¼	cup pecans, chopped, toasted

Peel the pears without removing stems. Combine the wine, lemon juice, lemon rind, sugar, cinnamon, and vanilla bean in a saucepan large enough to hold the pears comfortably. Add the pears and just enough water to cover the pears. Heat the mixture to a boil; reduce heat and simmer very slowly until the pears are just tender, 10 to 20 minutes.

Remove the pears to a plate and cool completely. Rapidly boil down liquid until it is reduced to 1 cup; strain.

To assemble, slice each pear in half vertically and scoop out the seeds, leaving a small circular hole. With a spoon, fill each half with mascarpone. On each serving plate, pour some of the reduced wine sauce to form a pool in the middle of the plate. Place two pear halves on each plate. Sprinkle the mascarpone with pecans. Drizzle the remaining red-wine sauce over the pears.

Makes 6 servings.

DINNER AT THE CASBAH

Orange and Olive Salad*

Moroccan Chicken*

Spiced Couscous with Vegetables*

Oven Roasted Root Vegetables

Fig Tart

WINE RECOMMENDATIONS:

White: A fragrant, young, unoaked Viognier

Red: Soft, ripe-fruited, low-tannin Merlot, Dolcetto, or Tempranillo

ORANGE AND OLIVE SALAD

Here is a favorite Moroccan salad recipe of mine, adapted from a recipe that appeared years ago in the Chicago Tribune. *The combination of the oranges and olives brings both color and flavor to the menu.*

—*Camilla Nielsen*

4   oranges (such as blood oranges, Valencias, *or* navel)

18 to 24 high-quality Mediterranean black olives, pitted, coarsely chopped

½   teaspoon ground cumin

¼   teaspoon sweet Hungarian paprika

Lettuce leaves for serving

Fresh parsley, minced, for garnish

Cut off the tops and bottoms of the oranges. Use a sharp knife to remove all the peels down to the flesh. Working over a bowl to catch the juices, cut between the membranes of the segments. Remove the seeds. Cut each segment into 3 pieces.

Combine the oranges with the olives, cumin, and paprika in a large bowl. Serve as is or place in lettuce-lined bowl. Garnish with parsley.

Makes 4 appetizer servings.

MOROCCAN CHICKEN

This is an easy recipe to prepare in advance. All the flavors taste great warm or at room temperature.
Plus, I am a firm believer that you can never have too many great chicken recipes. —*Carol Smoler*

- ½ cup olive oil, divided
- ¼ cup soy sauce
- ¼ cup sweet Marsala wine
- 1 tablespoon chopped garlic
- 2 teaspoons ground cumin
- 1 teaspoon paprika
- 1 chicken, cut into pieces, skin removed (about 3 to 4 pounds)
- 1 large onion, chopped
- ½ cup all-purpose flour
- 2 teaspoon ground cinnamon
- 1 teaspoon ground red pepper (cayenne)
- 1 teaspoon salt
- 2 lemons, thinly sliced

Combine ¼ cup of the olive oil, soy sauce, Marsala wine, garlic, cumin, and paprika in a large food-storage bag. Place the chicken in the bag. Close the bag and refrigerate the mixture overnight.

Preheat the oven to 350°F. Sauté the onion in 2 tablespoons of the remaining oil in a large well-seasoned or nonstick skillet until softened, about 5 minutes; set aside. Drain the chicken, reserving the marinade. Combine the flour, cinnamon, red pepper, and salt in shallow dish. Dredge the chicken in the flour mixture until lightly coated on all sides. Heat the remaining 2 tablespoons oil in the same skillet. Add the chicken in a single uncrowded layer. Cook until browned on both sides, about 10 minutes. Place the chicken in a baking dish. Top with the onions and reserved marinade.

Spread the sliced lemons over the chicken. Cover and bake until the chicken is no longer pink, about 45 minutes.

Makes 4 servings.

SPICED COUSCOUS WITH VEGETABLES

The seasonings of Moroccan cooking have always fascinated me. Their subtle blend of sweet, savory, and spicy flavors is refreshing in summer and comforting in winter. My students are always surprised by how quick and easy it is to simmer theses flavors with couscous. This fragrant and colorful side dish is my favorite complement to lamb and chicken.

—Madelaine Bullwinkel

2 tablespoons diced red onion
2 tablespoons diced yellow squash
2 tablespoons diced carrots
Olive oil
1 plum tomato, peeled and seeded, diced (retain juices)
½ teaspoon coarse sea salt
¼ teaspoon ground cinnamon
¼ teaspoon ground ginger
¼ teaspoon ground turmeric
⅛ teaspoon freshly ground pepper
1 cup couscous
¼ cup currants, *or* raisins (optional)
1½ cups water

Sauté the onion, yellow squash, and carrot in a small amount of olive oil in a large skillet over low heat, until vegetables begin to brown, about 10 minutes. Stir in the diced tomato, salt, and spices.

Add the couscous and currants; stir to coat. Add the water and retained tomato juices. Heat to a simmer, then turn off the heat. Cover and let the couscous stand 10 minutes. Fluff with a fork.

Makes 4 servings.

FOR THE BIG GAME

Red Devil Dip* with Crackers and Fresh Vegetable Dippers

Popcorn, Corn Chips, and Snack Mix

Assorted Sliced Meats and Cheeses

Savory Beef Stew with Roasted Vegetables*

Garlic and Blue Cheese Bread*

Brownies, Cookies, and M&Ms in Team Colors

WINE RECOMMENDATIONS:

Oak-aged, red-fruited Cabernet or Zinfandel with a few years of bottle age

RED DEVIL DIP

I serve this delicious dip at room temperature with Nicole's Divine Crackers—and I suggest trying it with our rye, salt, black pepper, garlic, or herb flavors. You may also use this dip in place of mayonnaise for turkey, roast-beef, chicken, or roasted-vegetable sandwiches.

—*Nicole Bergere*

1¼ cups diced seeded red bell peppers

2 packages (8 ounces each) cream cheese, cut into pieces

¼ cup sour cream

2 tablespoons unsalted butter, softened

1 teaspoon minced garlic

1 teaspoon Dijon-style mustard

½ teaspoon coarse (kosher) salt

⅛ teaspoon ground red pepper (cayenne)

1 teaspoon fresh lemon juice

1 jalapeño chili, seeded and thinly sliced

3 green onions, white and some green, quartered, thinly sliced

20 medium-size pimiento-stuffed olives, drained and sliced

Combine the red peppers with the cream cheese, sour cream, butter, garlic, and mustard in the bowl of a food processor. Process until smooth. Add the salt, red pepper, and lemon juice; process again until smooth. Transfer to a bowl and stir in the jalapeño chili, green onions, and olive slices. Cover and refrigerate 1 hour or more for flavors to meld. Adjust the seasonings to taste.

Makes about 3½ cups.

White bowl with matching platter for Bruschetta Bread from TFM.

SAVORY BEEF STEW WITH ROASTED VEGETABLES

This no-fuss recipe from the test kitchens of the National Cattlemen's Beef Association takes beef stew to the next level. The mélange of savory, tender beef with balsamic-infused roasted vegetables is party-perfect. And it's no-fuss—the beef simmers unattended, leaving time to roast the vegetables and prepare the accompaniments.

—Brenda McDowell

Recipe courtesy of National Cattlemen's Beef Association on behalf of The Beef Checkoff.

1¾ to 2 pounds boneless beef chuck shoulder, or bottom round
2½ tablespoon olive oil
3   cloves garlic, crushed
1   can (13¾ to 14½ ounces) ready-to-serve beef broth
¾   teaspoon freshly ground pepper
2   teaspoons dried thyme leaves
12 medium mushrooms
6   plum tomatoes, each cut lengthwise into quarters, seeded
3   small onions, each cut lengthwise into quarters
1½ tablespoons plus 2 teaspoons balsamic vinegar, divided
1   tablespoon cornstarch dissolved in 2 tablespoons water
    Fresh thyme, chopped (optional)

Trim the fat from the beef. Cut the beef into 1-inch pieces. Heat 1 tablespoon of the oil in a Dutch oven over medium heat until hot. Add half of the beef and garlic and brown evenly, stirring occasionally, about 10 minutes. Remove the browned meat to a plate and brown the remaining beef and garlic. Pour off the pan drippings. Return all the meat to the pot and add the broth, pepper, and dried thyme. Bring to a boil; reduce heat to low. Cover tightly and simmer, stirring occasionally, until the beef is fork-tender, 1½ to 2 hours.

Meanwhile, preheat the oven to 425°F. Lightly spray a jelly roll pan with nonstick cooking spray. Place the mushrooms, tomatoes, and onions in the pan. Combine the remaining 1½ tablespoons oil and 1½ tablespoons of the vinegar; drizzle the mixture over the vegetables, tossing to coat. Roast in 425°F oven until tender, 20 to 25 minutes.

Bring the beef stew to a boil over medium-high heat. Add the cornstarch mixture; cook and stir until the sauce is slightly thickened and bubbly, about 2 minutes. Stir in the roasted vegetables and the remaining 2 teaspoons vinegar. Sprinkle with fresh thyme, if desired.

Makes 6 servings.

GARLIC AND BLUE CHEESE BREAD

This party starter, which was created by my friend, entertainer extraordinaire and cookbook author Betty Rosbottom, always wins raves. I love it because it showcases two of my favorites—blue cheese and garlic —and it's extremely easy to assemble, can be made ahead, and the flavors are incredible.

—Brenda McDowell

½ cup (1 stick) butter

4 cloves garlic, finely chopped

1 loaf Italian bread, approximately 12 inches long

1 package (8 ounces) blue cheese, crumbled

1 small red onion, thinly sliced

Coarsely ground black pepper (optional)

12 kalamata olives, pitted and halved

1 teaspoon finely chopped fresh rosemary

Preheat the oven to 400°F. Melt the butter in a small saucepan over low heat. Stir in the garlic; set aside. Cut the bread lengthwise in half. Place the bread cut side up on an aluminum foil-lined baking sheet. Brush the cut sides with the garlic-butter mixture. Sprinkle with the cheese and onion. Season with pepper; sprinkle with the olives and rosemary. (Bread can be prepared up to this point in advance. Refrigerate, tightly covered, up to 24 hours.)

Bake until the cheese melts, 10 to 12 minutes (slightly longer if bread was refrigerated). Remove from the oven; cool 2 minutes. Cut into 1½ to 2 inch-wide slices; serve warm.

Makes 6 servings.

THANKSGIVING HARVEST FEAST

Mixed Green Salad with Pine Nuts and Pomegranate Seeds

Brined Turkey*

Cranberry Kumquat Conserve with Dried Cherries*

Albuquerque Corn*

Brussels Sprouts

Garlic Mashed Potatoes*

Brioche Dinner Rolls*

Rustic Pumpkin Tart*

WINE RECOMMENDATIONS:

White: Gewurztraminer or Riesling

Red: Cru Beaujolais or a refined, oak- and bottle-aged red wine

BRINED TURKEY

Several years ago, it became quite the "in" thing to brine your Thanksgiving turkey. I read article after article about it. I didn't really think it could make a difference but I gave it a try. I was amazed at the results; it was truly the best turkey I had ever made.

—Sara Reddington

4 quarts very cold water
1 cup coarse (kosher), *or* sea, salt
3 tablespoons granulated sugar
1 fresh, *or* thawed frozen, turkey (16 to 18 pounds)

Combine the water, salt and sugar; stir until the salt is dissolved. Place one large oven-cooking bag (or other large food-safe plastic bag) inside another; place the bags in a shallow roasting pan. Place the turkey in the bag, breast side down.

Carefully pour the salt mixture over the turkey inside the bag. Secure the inner bag tightly over the turkey; secure the outer bag tightly as well. Refrigerate the turkey in the brine for 12 to 18 hours. Remove the turkey from the brine; rinse well. Pat the turkey dry with paper towels. (The turkey can be refrigerated until ready to cook for up to 24 hours).

Preheat the oven to 325°F. Turn the wings back to hold the neck skin against the back of the turkey. Place the turkey, breast side up, in a shallow roasting pan.

Bake until a meat thermometer inserted in the thigh reaches 165°F, 3 to 3½ hours. Loosely cover the breast and tops of drumsticks with aluminum foil if they begin to get too brown. Let the turkey stand 15 minutes before carving.

Makes 12 to 14 servings.

CRANBERRY KUMQUAT CONSERVE WITH DRIED CHERRIES

The Butterball Turkey Talk-Line started in 1981. I was the director and internal implementer of the concept from its inception, and I continued as its corporate spokesperson for nearly 10 years. I have so many stories— it was a truly fabulous time—and I am so proud of the sustainability of the program. This is a recipe from one of the many brochures produced for the Talk-Line.

—Nancy Rodriguez

3	cups fresh, or frozen, cranberries
¾	cup port wine
1½	cups kumquats, *or* 1 medium orange, quartered, seeded
2½	cups packed light brown sugar
1½	cups dried tart red cherries, *or* 1 can (16 ounces) tart red cherries, drained
¼	cup cider vinegar
1	teaspoon ground cinnamon
¼	teaspoon salt
¼	teaspoon ground ginger
¼	teaspoon ground cloves

Combine the cranberries and wine in a large saucepan. Bring to a boil over high heat. Reduce heat to low; cover and simmer until the cranberry skins pop, 8 to 10 minutes. Meanwhile, coarsely chop the kumquats or the orange in a blender or food processor. Add the kumquats to the cranberries. Stir in the brown sugar, dried cherries, vinegar, cinnamon, salt, ginger, and cloves. Simmer, uncovered, over medium heat until the mixture thickens nicely, 30 to 35 minutes. Cool. Spoon conserve into containers. Store in the refrigerator.

Makes 8 to 10 servings (about 2½ cups).

ALBUQUERQUE CORN

The addition of jalapeño chili and cumin give this side dish the irresistible flavors of the Southwest.

—*Abby Mandel*

2	tablespoons extra virgin olive oil
4	large ears of corn, kernels cut off, about 2 cups
½	jalapeño chili, seeded and minced
1	small jicama, about 10 ounces, peeled and chopped (about 2 cups)
8	green onions, thinly sliced (about 1 cup)
½	teaspoon ground cumin
½	teaspoon salt

Heat the oil in a 12-inch nonstick skillet over medium-high heat. When hot, add the corn and jalapeño pepper. Cook, stirring often, until the corn is hot, about 2 minutes. Add the jicama, onions, cumin, and salt. Heat thoroughly, stirring occasionally, about 2 more minutes. Adjust the seasoning. Serve hot or at room temperature.

Makes 6 servings.

GARLIC MASHED POTATOES

I prefer to use red-skinned potatoes when mashing, but Yukon Golds are an excellent alternative. Russets will produce a drier, fluffier texture. It's up to you. Regardless, potatoes and garlic are a delicious pairing.

—Jill Van Cleave

3	pounds potatoes, peeled and quartered, *or* cut into large chunks
20 to 24	medium-sized cloves garlic, peeled (about 1 head)
1	teaspoon salt, *or* more to taste
6	tablespoons unsalted butter, softened
½	cup heavy (whipping) cream
½	teaspoon ground white pepper

Place the potato chunks and garlic cloves in a large saucepan. Cover with cold water by an inch or so. Bring to a boil over medium-high heat, and add a little salt. Cook at a medium boil until the potatoes test very tender, about 20 minutes.

Remove the pan from heat and reserve ½ cup of the cooking water; set aside. Drain the potatoes and garlic in a colander.

Place the butter and cream in a mixing bowl. Using a ricer, push the potatoes and garlic through it into the bowl. Add hot cooking water to the potato-garlic mash. Stir vigorously until smooth, adding the salt and white pepper. Taste and adjust the seasonings.

Makes 8 to 10 servings.

Notes

If a ricer is not available, return the drained potatoes to the same pot; add the butter, cream, reserved water, salt, and pepper, and mash the potatoes with a handheld potato masher to the desired consistency.

Do not use a food processor with cooked potatoes.

BRIOCHE DINNER ROLLS

Pamela Fitzpatrick is the executive baker at Fox & Obel food market, where these rolls are sold. "I find brioche to be one of the most flexible doughs," she says. "It is sturdy enough to withstand the addition of cheeses, onions, peppers, etc., and it can be used for all kinds of savory breads. In sweet applications, brioche rolls transform into breakfast buns by a simple sprinkling of sugar, by pressing berries into the dough, or by spreading the tops of buns with frangipane before baking. The rich dough is also interesting enough to stand on its own as in these delicious dinner rolls."

— *Pamela Fitzpatrick*

SPONGE:

- ¾ cup water
- ⅓ cup whole milk
- 1¼ teaspoons (⅛ ounce) dry yeast
- 2 cups all-purpose flour

DOUGH:

- 4 large eggs, at room temperature
- 3½ cups all-purpose flour
- 1¼ teaspoons (⅛ ounce) dry yeast
- ½ cup granulated sugar
- 1 cup (2 sticks or 8 ounces) butter (preferably a high-fat butter such as Plugra brand), softened, cut into slices
- 2½ teaspoons salt

For the sponge, combine the ingredients in a large bowl and mix into a smooth, wet dough. Let stand at room temperature, covered, overnight.

For the dough, combine the sponge with the eggs, flour, yeast, and sugar in the large bowl of an electric mixer. Mix on low speed, using the dough hook attachment, for 1 minute.

Add the butter and continue to mix on low speed for 1 minute. Turn the mixer off and let the dough rest 10 minutes. Add the salt and mix on medium-low speed for 4 minutes. Finish mixing on medium-high speed until the dough is smooth, about 4 to 6 minutes. (The dough's temperature should be 73°F to 74°F.) Place the dough in a floured bowl and cover. Let rise at room temperature until the bulk doubles, about 2 hours. Divide the dough in half and let rest for 10 minutes.

To shape, turn the dough halves onto a floured surface and roll them into 2 ropes, each about 3 inches thick. Cut each rope into 10 equal pieces and roll each piece into a ball. Place the shaped pieces on two parchment-lined baking sheets (about 10 rolls per pan). Cover and let rise 30 minutes before baking.

Preheat the oven to 325°F. Bake until lightly browned, about 20 minutes. Cool on a wire rack. Serve warm.

Makes 20 rolls.

RUSTIC PUMPKIN TART

While I love fresh pumpkin custard pies for the holidays, this recipe is something different and much more casual—a great combination of ginger and pumpkin that shows off the delicate flavor of the squash in the filling.

— Pamela Fitzpatrick

GINGERBREAD COOKIE CRUST: :

- ½ cup (1 stick) unsalted butter, softened
- ⅓ cup packed dark brown sugar
- 3 tablespoons mild unsulphured molasses
- 2 tablespoons finely chopped crystallized ginger
- 1¼ cups all-purpose flour
- ⅓ cup whole wheat flour
- 1 teaspoon ground ginger
- ½ teaspoon ground cinnamon
- ¼ teaspoon baking soda
- ¼ teaspoon salt

PUMPKIN FILLING:

- 1 can (15 ounces) solid-packed pumpkin
- ½ cup packed dark brown sugar
- 1 egg
- ½ teaspoon ground cinnamon
- ¼ teaspoon ground allspice
- ¼ teaspoon ground ginger
- ⅓ cup heavy (whipping) cream
- 3 tablespoons apricot preserves, melted
- 3 tablespoons pumpkin seeds (*pepitas*), chopped, toasted

For the gingerbread cookie crust, spray a 10-inch round tart pan with a removable bottom with nonstick cooking spray; set aside. Preheat the oven to 400°F. Cream the butter and sugar with the paddle of an electric mixer. Add the molasses and crystallized ginger; beat well. Combine the dry ingredients in a medium bowl. Add to the creamed mixture in two batches, beating well between each addition. (The mixture will be crumbly.) Spoon the crust mixture in an even layer into the tart pan. Press firmly onto the bottom and up sides to form the crust. Lay a piece of parchment paper on top of the crust; top with pie weights. Bake 10 minutes. Remove the parchment and weights. Prick the crust with a fork. Continue baking until the bottom of the crust has lost its sheen and is set, 6 to 8 minutes. Remove from the oven to a cooling rack.

Reduce the oven temperature to 350°F.

For the pumpkin filling, whisk together the pumpkin, sugar, egg, and spices in a large bowl until well blended. Whisk in the cream. Pour into the warm crust. Smooth the top with a spatula. Bake until the filling is just set, about 30 minutes. Cool completely on a wire rack.

Before serving, remove the sides of the tart pan. Brush melted preserves over the top of the tart. Sprinkle the chopped pepitas around the edge of the tart. Cut into wedges to serve. Store the leftovers, tightly wrapped, in the refrigerator.

Makes 8 to 10 servings (one 10-inch tart).

HOLIDAY COCKTAIL PARTY

Cheese Sticks*

Vegetable Crudités and Dip

Assorted Olives and Marinated Cheese Cubes

Spicy Crab and Shrimp Rolls with Salsa*

Cinnamon and Sugar Pecans*

WINE RECOMMENDATIONS:

Sparkling: Prosecco

White: Gewurztraminer or an off-dry Riesling

CHEESE STICKS

Cooking a meal for family or friends on their turf requires thinking like a caterer. I have at least a dozen memories of toting prepared and semi-prepared foods to the Gold Coast home of Marian Tripp, a founding member of our Les Dames chapter and the owner of Marian Tripp Communications. Marian shared a summertime birthday with my husband, Bill Rice, a well-known food and wine journalist and longtime friend of Marian's. Although Bill would do much of the meal preparation while I did the baking, there were two reasons why our celebratory meal was carried out in an easy-to-complete state: Marian's kitchen was tiny, and it was usually sweltering hot in Chicago at the end of July. No one wanted to turn on burners or an oven for very long.

This cheese pastry produces finger food appetizer sticks that are perfectly suited to casual entertaining and great for making ahead. The recipe is adapted from a cookbook I wrote called The Neighborhood Bakeshop, *which was published by William Morrow in 1997. The original recipe from the owners of the Palo Alto Baking Co. in California uses homemade quick-style puff pastry dough. Here, I suggest substituting a good-quality, store-bought prepared frozen puff pastry—preferably one made with real butter. When baked, the result is crisp, flaky, and savory cheese sticks that are perfect with cocktails or wine.* —Jill Van Cleave

1¾ cups cake flour
1   cup shredded Swiss cheese
¾   cup plus ⅓ cup grated Parmesan cheese
¾   cup (1½ sticks) unsalted butter, chilled, cut into small pieces
1   cup heavy (whipping) cream, chilled
1   sheet (10-inches square) thawed frozen puff pastry dough, chilled (half of 1.1-pound package)

Combine the cake flour, Swiss cheese, and ¾ cup of the Parmesan cheese in a large mixing bowl; stir to mix thoroughly. Cut in the butter with a pastry blender until the mixture is crumbly. Add the cream; stir to form a moist dough. Wrap the dough completely in waxed paper and refrigerate until firm, at least 1 hour. (The dough may be prepared in advance and refrigerated overnight.)

Sprinkle your work surface lightly with flour and roll out the puff pastry dough into a 10 x 18-inch rectangle. On a separate lightly floured board, roll out the cheese pastry dough into a 10-inch square. Place the cheese pastry square on top of the puff pastry to cover it by two-thirds. Fold the uncovered flap of the puff pastry over the cheese, then fold the opposite end over to cover the filling completely. Wrap in plastic wrap and refrigerate at least 30 minutes.

Return the chilled, folded dough to the lightly floured work surface. Roll out into a 10 x 15-inch rectangle. Fold a short end over to cover one-third of the rectangle, then fold the opposite end over to cover it completely. Wrap again in plastic wrap and refrigerate for 30 minutes more.

Return the dough to a lightly floured work surface and roll out into an 8 x 18-inch rectangle, about ¼-inch thickness. Cut crosswise strips, ½-inch wide. Twist each strip tightly into a spiral shape, pushing on each end to flatten slightly. Place 1-inch apart on parchment-lined baking sheets. Sprinkle the twists with the remaining ⅓ cup Parmesan cheese. Set aside, or refrigerate until ready to bake.

Preheat the oven to 350°F. Bake the pastry twists until lightly golden, 25 minutes. Reduce the oven temperature to 300°F. Continue to bake until golden and crisp, about 15 minutes more. Remove from the pans to wire racks to cool.

Makes 32 to 36 pastries (about 12 appetizer servings).

SPICY CRAB AND SHRIMP ROLLS WITH SALSA

At Frontera Foods, we are always figuring out ways to use our fire-roasted salsas. I love the combination of seafood and salsa. These crispy, finger-size rolls are reminiscent of the seafood empanadas sold by bicycle vendors along the waterfront in Veracruz. They are great for entertaining because they can be prepared up to 1 day in advance of serving: Simply shape the rolls, arrange them in a single layer on a buttered baking sheet, and refrigerate, tightly covered. Bake just before serving. Serve the rolls warm with more salsa.

—JeanMarie Brownson

2 tablespoons olive oil	⅛ teaspoon saffron threads
½ pound uncooked medium-size shrimp, peeled and deveined	¼ cup chopped fresh Italian parsley
½ pound lump crabmeat	⅓ cup chopped fresh cilantro
1 cup fire-roasted tomato salsa	About ½ cup fresh bread crumbs (not dry)
⅓ cup finely chopped white onion	Salt, to taste
2 cloves garlic, finely chopped	½ pound phyllo (filo) dough, thawed according to the package directions
1 teaspoon imported sweet paprika	½ cup (1 stick) unsalted butter, melted
½ teaspoon ground cumin	¼ cup extra virgin olive oil
¼ to ½ teaspoon ground red pepper (cayenne) to taste	Cilantro sprigs for garnish
	Fire-roasted tomato salsa for serving

Heat the olive oil in a skillet over medium heat. Add the shrimp and cook, stirring occasionally, until they begin to turn pink and are cooked through, about 2 minutes. Transfer the shrimp to a cutting board, leaving any excess oil in the pan; chop coarsely and put into a bowl. Mix in the crabmeat and set aside.

Return the pan to medium-low heat. Add the salsa, onion, garlic, paprika, cumin, cayenne pepper, and saffron, and stir to mix well. Simmer slowly, stirring occasionally, until most of the moisture has evaporated, 5 to 10 minutes. Stir the mixture into the shrimp and crab. Add the parsley, cilantro, and enough of the bread crumbs to make a fairly dry mixture. Mix well and season with salt to taste.

Preheat the oven to 400°F. Lightly butter 2 baking sheets. (CONTINUED ON NEXT PAGE)

Place the phyllo sheets in a neat stack on the cutting board, with the long edges facing you. Cut the stack crosswise into quarters, forming strips about 4 inches wide. Cover with a dampened kitchen towel until ready to use. Always keep the phyllo covered while you are working.

Mix the melted butter and olive oil. Brush 1 phyllo strip very lightly with the butter mixture, and place a second strip on top. Brush the second strip lightly with the butter mixture. Place a heaping teaspoonful of filling along the short end nearest you. Fold in the sides of the phyllo to somewhat enclose the filling and then roll up to form a cigar shape. Place on a prepared baking sheet and brush lightly with the butter mixture. Repeat with the remaining phyllo and filling.

Bake until golden, about 15 minutes. Transfer to a platter and garnish with cilantro sprigs. Serve immediately with more salsa for dipping.

Makes about 40 rolls (about 10 to 12 appetizer servings).

CINNAMON AND SUGAR PECANS

This is a favorite snack in our house for the holidays—one of those treats you can't stop eating. It's perfect for gift giving. The crunchy nuts go great with Champagne or dessert wine, too!   —*Diane Kase Sokolofski*

1	egg white
1	tablespoon water
1	pound pecan halves
1	cup granulated sugar
1	teaspoon ground cinnamon
1	teaspoon salt
6	tablespoons butter, melted

Preheat the oven to 300°F. Butter a 15 x 12-inch jelly roll pan. Beat the egg white and water until frothy. Add the pecans and toss to coat. Combine the sugar, cinnamon, and salt in a large bowl. Toss the pecans in the sugar mixture to coat evenly. Spread in a single layer on the prepared jelly roll pan. Drizzle with the melted butter.

Bake, stirring every 15 minutes, until deep golden brown and crisp, 45 to 60 minutes, Remove from the oven and spread on brown paper in a single layer. Let cool. Store in resealable plastic bags.

Makes 6 to 8 servings (about 1 pound).

ELEGANT CHRISTMAS DINNER

Oyster Saffron Bisque*

Sun-Dried Tomato Stuffed Beef Tenderloin*

Rice Pilaf

Oven Roasted Brussels Sprouts

Winter Fruit Dessert*

WINE RECOMMENDATIONS:

For first course: The dry Chenin of Loire or cool-climate Savennieres

For main course: A fruit-forward red with earthy notes:
Napa Cabernet or a Zinfandel with a few years age

For dessert: Malmsey Madeira or aged Tawny Porto

OYSTER SAFFRON BISQUE

In 1983, one of Les Dames' charter members, Leslee Reis, appeared on Julia Child's TV show to demonstrate an oyster-on-the-half-shell preparation that featured carrots. Because my book Oysters: A Culinary Celebration was soon to be published, I wrote to Leslee and remarked on the coincidence. She graciously said that after I settled in my new home in Lake Forest (I moved from Cape Cod), she would introduce me to Les Dames Chicago. Unfortunately, her untimely death and my own time constraints postponed my induction until 1997, and I never really got to know Leslee. Still, the pairing of carrots and oysters is most unusual. I don't have her recipe, but here's mine. It is essential to use freshly shucked oysters for the ultimate flavor.   —Joan Reardon

24 oysters, freshly shucked, with their liquor (about 1 pound or 1 pint)

3 medium carrots

4 tablespoons butter

1 cup chopped celery

1 cup chopped onion

6 cups vegetable stock

1½ cups peeled, diced potato

½ lemon

2 tablespoons chopped fresh dill weed, plus more for garnish

1 teaspoon saffron threads, crushed

1 cup heavy (whipping) cream

Salt and freshly ground white pepper, to taste

Strain the oysters, reserving the liquor. Peel the carrots and chop 2 of them for the soup; set aside. Cut the remaining carrot into fine julienne strips and blanch it in boiling salted water. Rinse in cold water; drain and reserve it for garnish.

Melt the butter in a large saucepan and sauté the chopped carrots, celery, and onion until tender, about 15 minutes. Add the oyster liquor, stock, potato, lemon, dill, and saffron. Bring to a boil; cover and simmer until the vegetables are very tender, about 15 minutes. Remove the lemon and purée the vegetable mixture (in batches) in a food processor or blender. Transfer the puréed vegetables back to the saucepan; add the cream and heat to a boil. Add the oysters and heat gently, just until their edges begin to curl, about 3 minutes. Season to taste with salt and pepper.

Ladle into shallow soup bowls and garnish with julienned carrots and snipped dill; serve immediately.

Makes 8 servings.

THE PROPER OYSTER

A part of America's dining scene since New England's Wampanoag tribe introduced them to the first settlers, oysters sustained American colonists along the Eastern seaboard during food shortages. Oysters became the piece de resistance of fine dining from the late 19th century to the present. An oyster craze spread across America to Chicago via "oyster wagons" that crossed the Alleghenies to Pittsburgh; the oysters then traveled by boat, after the Erie Barge Canal opened, or by rail after the railroads moved westward. Oysters were rushed to the oyster cellars, saloons, and bars of Chicago. Politicians frequently plotted their strategies over platters of raw oysters and glasses of beer in Chicago's early oyster bars.

Here are tips for entertaining with oysters:

- Six raw oysters per person are usually served as a first course. Because of their small size, however, an appropriate serving of Kumamoto oysters would be 8 or 10. If the oysters are larger than 3 inches and they are baked or broiled with a rich sauce or dressing, 3 or 4 per person are usually recommended.

- Oysters can never be undercooked, but can be ruined by overcooking, which toughens them and diminishes their flavor. When baking an oyster appetizer, use a hot oven (400 to 450 degrees) unless the other ingredients dictate a lower temperature. When broiling, place the pan 4 inches from the heat and cook for less than 5 minutes. When poaching an oyster, cook it only until it is plump or until its edges begin to curl, and then remove it from the heat.

—Joan Reardon

SUN-DRIED TOMATO STUFFED BEEF TENDERLOIN

Beef tenderloin is my number one choice for entertaining, and this versatile recipe is one of my favorites. Created by beef experts, it stands alone as a fantastic roast, but works just as well as a starter, carved thinly and served on crostini. For sandwiches, add caramelized onions and goat cheese—there's none better!

—*Brenda McDowell*

Recipe courtesy of National Cattlemen's Beef Association on behalf of The Beef Checkoff.

1 center-cut beef tenderloin roast (2 to 3 pounds), not tied
⅓ cup sun-dried tomato spread
2 tablespoons finely chopped parsley

Preheat the oven to 425°F. Make a horizontal cut through the center of the beef roast, parallel to the surface of the meat. Cut to, but not through, the opposite side. Open the meat so it lies flat, like an open book.

Combine the sun-dried tomato spread and parsley in a small bowl. Spread it lengthwise over half of the meat. Fold the other half of the meat over to form the original shape of the roast. Tie at 1½- to 2-inch intervals with kitchen twine and trim off any excess twine.

Place the roast on a rack in a shallow roasting pan. Insert an ovenproof meat thermometer so the tip is centered in the thickest part of the beef, not resting in fat. Roast until the meat thermometer registers 135°F, 30 to 40 minutes. Transfer the roast to a carving board; tent loosely with aluminum foil. Let stand 10 minutes before slicing. (The temperature will continue to rise about 10°F, to reach 145°F for medium rare.) Serve thinly sliced.

Makes 8 servings.

WINTER FRUIT DESSERT

The first time I made this recipe was for a Les Dames holiday party. It was very well received, so by popular request, I shared the recipe with the group via our newsletter.   —*Queenie Burns*

1½ cups water

½   cup granulated sugar

1   package (7 ounces) mixed dried fruits (prunes, pears, apricots, peaches, apples, and figs),
     cut into ½-inch pieces

½   cup dried cherries, or cranberries

¼   cup raisins

½   cup fresh orange juice

½   cup sweet white wine, such as Riesling

¼   teaspoon ground cinnamon

4   whole, or ⅛ teaspoon ground, cloves

½   cup seedless grapes

8   slices pound cake
     Sweetened whipped cream (optional)
     Orange and lemon slices, for garnish

Combine the water and sugar in a large saucepan; cook and stir over medium heat until the sugar dissolves. Add the dried fruits, dried cherries, raisins, orange juice, wine, cinnamon, and cloves. Heat to a boil. Reduce heat and simmer until the fruits are tender and the liquid is reduced to a syrup, about 20 minutes. Stir in the grapes. Cool; discard the cloves.

Serve warm or at room temperature over the pound cake and topped with whipped cream, if desired. Garnish with the orange and lemon slices.

Makes 8 servings.

Note
The fruit mixture can be prepared and refrigerated up to 3 days ahead.

APPENDICES

2007 LES DAMES D'ESCOFFIER MEMBERSHIP LIST

Jennifer A. Anderson, president, Jennifer Anderson & Associates; events/conference planner; www.JenniferAndersonEvents.com

Maria Battaglia, president, LaCucina Italiana; chef; recipe developer; educator; www.la-cucina-italiana.com

Deann Groen Bayless, co-owner, Frontera Grill and Topolobampo restaurants; www.rickbayless.com

Dana Benigno, owner/chef, Chicago Cooks culinary instruction website; www.chicagocooks.com

Nicole Bergere, owner/chef, Nicole's, Inc. specialty crackers and bakery; www.nicolescrackers.com

JeanMarie Brownson, culinary director/owner, Frontera Foods, Inc.; www.fronterakitchens.com

Nancy Brussat Barocci, owner, Convito Café & Market; www.convitocafeandmarket.com

Madelaine Bullwinkel, owner, Chez Madelaine Cooking School; www.chezm.com

Queenie Burns, corporate design director, Marketing and Technology Group trade magazines, www.marketingandtechnology.com

Carolyn Collins, president, Collins Caviar Company; www.collinscaviar.com

Maria Josefa Concannon, owner, Don Juan's Restaurante; www.donjuanschicago.com

Judy Contino, owner, Bittersweet Bakery; www.bittersweetpastry.com

Mariana Coyne, farm forager; documentary journalist; local food system development specialist

Debra Crestoni, owner, Connoisseur Wines; importer; exporter

Priscilla Cretier, co-owner/manager, Le Vichyssois Restaurant; www.levichyssois.com

Ann Flanagan Doppes, co-owner, Bistrot Margot; www.bistrotmargot.com

Toria O. Emas, administration director, Chicago Bar Association; private club, events, and conference planner; www.chicagobar.org

Patricia Penzey Erd, co-owner, The Spice House specialty food retailer; educator; www.thespicehouse.com

Pamela Sue Fitzpatrick, executive baker, Fox & Obel food market/bakery; www.fox-obel.com

Suzanne Florek, chef, recipe developer, product developer, Whisk Inc.

Gale Gand, executive pastry chef/partner, TRU/Cenitare Restaurants; author; TV host/producer; www.trurestaurant.com; www.cenitare.com

Sue Ling Gin, chairman, Flying Food Fare, Inc., inflight catering and foodservice; www.flyingfood.com

Barbara Glunz-Donovan, proprietor, The House of Glunz Wine Shop; educator; wine writer; www.houseofglunz.com

Elaine González, consultant, Chocolate Artistry; vocational culinary educator; author; www.elainegonzalez.com

Linda J. Goodman, president, Linda Goodman & Co.; events, conference planner

Barbara S. Gorham, owner, Margarita European Inn; www.margaritainn.com

Della Gossett, pastry chef, Charlie Trotter's restaurant; www.charlietrotters.com

Rita E. Gutekanst, owner, Limelight Catering; www.limelightcatering.com

Carol Mighton Haddix, food editor, *Chicago Tribune*; freelance writer/editor; www.chicagotribune.com

Nancy Kirby Harris, senior executive director, American Diabetes Association; www.diabetes.org

Mary Abbott Hess, LHD, MS, RD, LD, FADA, president, Culinary Nutrition Associates; partner, Hess & Hunt, Inc. Nutrition Communications; consultant; author; publisher; www.culinarynutritionassociates.com

Judith Dunbar Hines, director of culinary arts & events, City of Chicago Department of Cultural Affairs; conference planner; www.cityofchicago.org/culturalaffairs

Meme Hopmayer, partner/market specialist, Fox & Obel food market; www.fox-obel.com

En-Ming Hsu, executive pastry chef, Four Seasons Hotels; consultant; www.fourseasons.com

Elizabeth A. Karmel, creator/owner, Girls at the Grill® and Grill Friends™; author; www.GirlsattheGrill.com; www.GrillFriends.com

Kristin James, lawyer, Cuisine & Culture International, Ltd.; founder of Prairie Kitchens Cooking School; www.prairiekitchens.com

Alma Lach, president, Alma Lach, Inc.; author; food consultant; www.almalach.com

Karen Levin, food consultant; cookbook author; recipe developer and tester; food writer

Lois Carol Levine, food consultant; educator

Joyce Lofstrom, corporate communications manager, HIMSS; public relations; www.himss.org

Jeanne McInerney-Lubeck, owner, Bamboo Blue restaurant; retail sales; www.bambooblue.biz

Norma Maloney, vice president of sales & special events, Lettuce Entertain You Enterprises, conference planner; www.leye.com

Abby Mandel, founder/president, Chicago's Green City Market, local sustainable farmers market; www.chicagogreencitymarket.org

Brenda McDowell, owner, M&P Food Communications, public relations firm; www.mpfood.com

Mary Elizabeth McMahon, pastry chef

Michaele Musel, associate director, Beef Demonstration Center, National Cattlemen's Beef Association; www.beef.org

Carrie Nahabedian, co-owner/chef, NAHA restaurant; www.naha-chicago.com

Camilla Nielsen, chairman of the board, Nielsen-Massey Vanillas; Flavor House; www.nielsenmassey.com

Wendy Pashman, president, The Entertaining Company, catering firm; www.entertainingcompany.com

Lisa Piasecki-Rosskamm, president, Lisa Piasecki-Rosskamm Food & Nutrition Consultants, Inc., food marketing communications

Donna Pierce, staff writer/test kitchen director, *Chicago Tribune*; freelance writer/editor; www.chicagotribune.com

Ina Pinkney, co-owner, Ina's Kitchen restaurant; pastry chef; www.breakfastqueen.com

Joan Reardon, writer; cookbook author; biographer; editor; culinary historian

Pamela Reardon, president, Raspberry Island specialty foods; www.raspberryisland.net

Sara Armstrong Reddington, senior account manager, M&P Food Communications, public relations firm; www.mpfood.com

Nancy Rodriguez, president, Food Marketing Support Services, Inc., food product design; www.fmssinc.com

Katheryn Ruff, president, Tablescapes Party Rental; www.tablescapes.com

Joan Saltzman, personal chef, caterer

Reysa Samuels, gourmet foods and cheese retail sales/consultant, Sam's Wines & Spirits retail store; www.samswine.com

Sylvia Schur, founder, Creative Food Services; food journalist; food consultant

Carole Browe Segal, vice president of civic affairs, Crate & Barrel retail stores; www.CrateandBarrel.com

Debra Sharpe, owner, Feast, Cru Café and Wine Bar, and Half & Half restaurants, and The Goddess and Grocer retail store; www.goddessandgrocer.com

Nancy Siler, vice president of consumer affairs, Wilton Industries, Inc., public relations firm; www.wilton.com, www.bakedecoratecelebrate.com

Katherine Smith, principal, Smith Partners, food and marketing communications

Carol Smoler, food stylist; recipe developer; consultant; www.smolerfoodstylist.com

Diane Sokoloski, senior manager, Kraft Foods; food editor for *Comida y Familia*, a Hispanic food magazine; www.kraft.com

Sofia Solomon, president, TEKLA, Inc., importer, distributor and wholesaler of specialty foods; www.winecheese.com

Camille Janet Stagg, president, Camille Stagg & Associates; food, wine, and travel journalist; consultant; teacher

Sarah Stegner, co-owner/chef, Prairie Grass Restaurant; www.prairiegrasscafe.com

Jill Van Cleave, president, Jill Van Cleave Ltd.; recipe developer and tester; staff writer; editor; www.foodchic.com

Candace Barocci Warner, general manager, Convito Café & Market, Italian food/wine market and restaurant; www.convitocafeandmarket.com

Marilyn Jo Wilkinson, director, National Product Communications, Wisconsin Milk Marketing Board; www.wisdairy.com

BIBLIOGRAPHY

Bundy, Beverly. *The Century in Food: America's Fads and Favorites*. Collector's Press, 2002.

Great Chefs. *Great Chefs of Chicago*. Tele-record Productions, Avon Books Ltd., 1985.

Grossman, James R., Keating, Ann Durkin, and Reiff, Janice L. *The Encyclopedia of Chicago*. University of Chicago Press, 2004.

Grunes, Barbara. *Dining In—Chicago Vol. 2*. Peanut Butter Publishing, 1982.

Kamp, David. *The United States of Arugula.* Broadway Books, 2006.

Kaplan, Sherman. *Best Restaurants Chicago.*101 Productions, 1986.

Lovegren, Sylvia. *Fashionable Food: Seven Decades of Food Fads.* The University of Chicago Press, 1995, 2005.

Matasar, Ann B. *Women of Wine: The Rise of Women in the Global Wine Industry.* University of California Press, 2006.

Rice, William, and Wolf, Burton, eds. *Where to Eat in America*, New Edition. Random House, 1979.

Smith, Andrew F., ed. *The Oxford Encyclopedia of Food and Drink in America.* Oxford University Press, 2004.

Stevens, Karen Goldwach. *Dining In—Chicago Vol. 1*. Peanut Butter Publishing, 1979.

Traeger, James. *The Food Chronology*. Owl Books, 1995.

Zagat. *Zagat Survey, Chicago Restaurants*. Zagat Survey LLC, 2005/2006.

PEOPLE AND PLACES INDEX

Recipes are indicated by an R after the page number, and Sidebars are indicated by an S.

PEOPLE

A

B

C

D

E

GENERAL INDEX

Sidebars are indicated by an S after the page number.